Test-Driven Development with React

Apply Test-Driven Development in Your Applications

Juntao Qiu

Test-Driven Development with React

Juntao Qiu
Burwood East, 3151, Victoria, Australia

ISBN-13 (pbk): 978-1-4842-6971-8   ISBN-13 (electronic): 978-1-4842-6972-5
https://doi.org/10.1007/978-1-4842-6972-5

Managing Director, Apress Media LLC: Welmoed Spahr
Acquisitions Editor: Louise Corrigan
Development Editor: James Markham
Coordinating Editor: Nancy Chen

Cover designed by eStudioCalamar

Cover image designed by Freepik (www.freepik.com)

Distributed to the book trade worldwide by Springer Science+Business Media New York, 1 New York Plaza, New York, NY 10004. Phone 1-800-SPRINGER, fax (201) 348-4505, e-mail orders-ny@springer-sbm.com, or visit www.springeronline.com. Apress Media, LLC is a California LLC and the sole member (owner) is Springer Science + Business Media Finance Inc (SSBM Finance Inc). SSBM Finance Inc is a **Delaware** corporation.

For information on translations, please e-mail booktranslations@springernature.com; for reprint, paperback, or audio rights, please e-mail bookpermissions@springernature.com.

Apress titles may be purchased in bulk for academic, corporate, or promotional use. eBook versions and licenses are also available for most titles. For more information, reference our Print and eBook Bulk Sales web page at http://www.apress.com/bulk-sales.

Any source code or other supplementary material referenced by the author in this book is available to readers on GitHub via the book's product page, located at www.apress.com/9781484269718. For more detailed information, please visit http://www.apress.com/source-code.

Printed on acid-free paper

For my wife Mansi and daughter Luna

Table of Contents

About the Author

Juntao Qiu is a senior web application developer at ThoughtWorks. Over the past ten years, he has helped his clients to build solid, extensible, and high-quality web applications on a range of projects including traditional web applications using jQuery and JSP (Java Server Pages) to single-page applications (SPAs) using Backbone, AngularJS, and React. Juntao knows how to handle the complexity of real-world projects by applying appropriate methodologies including writing clean code and effective automation tests. He also is a technical author who has already published two books in the Chinese language: *JavaScript Core Concepts and Practices* (2013) and *Lightweight Web Application Development* (2015). He is passionate about writing blogs and speaking at events. He has a real passion for clean code, refactoring, and Test-Driven Development. Additionally, he does Muay Thai and boxing in his spare time.

About the Technical Reviewer

 **Alexander Chinedu Nnakwue** has a background in Mechanical Engineering from the University of Ibadan, Nigeria, and has been a front-end developer for over three years working on both web and mobile technologies. He also has experience as a technical author, writer, and reviewer. He enjoys programming for the Web, and occasionally, you can also find him playing soccer. He was born in Benin City and is currently based in Lagos, Nigeria.

Foreword

Sometimes, I find it hard to believe that it's been more than two decades since Kent Beck published *Extreme Programming Explained* including Test-Driven Development as a core practice. In the years since then, the use of automated testing has become quite commonplace, something that almost all developers are familiar with – however, the "red-green-refactor" cycle of TDD is often missing. The reality is that building software test first is not easy or trivial in real-world software development and requires deliberate practice and usually someone experienced to learn from.

At ThoughtWorks, my role is Head of Engineering – responsible for the quality of the software that our teams produce for and with our clients. We set a high standard for the "internal" quality of the code we produce, wanting it to be maintainable and extensible so that it can quickly be changed with confidence. Test-Driven Development is a default practice in ThoughtWorks – our experience shows that the practice leads to better software design and good confidence from a comprehensive automated test suite.

In my years at ThoughtWorks, I've seen the phenomenal rise in the importance of JavaScript and browser applications. In 2010, we advised that the industry should treat JavaScript as a first-class language (`www.thoughtworks.com/radar/languages--and-frameworks/javascript-as-a-first-class-language`) on the ThoughtWorks Technology Radar, applying all of the same engineering rigor as other platforms. As one of the authors of the Technology Radar, I've seen and helped document the explosion of tooling and frameworks in JavaScript, many of which have been related to the area of test automation.

Test-Driven Development with React is a practical and hands-on guide to learn TDD with React, the most prevalent browser application framework in use today. It guides the reader through the fundamentals of TDD with React by implementing a series of requirements in a nontrivial example application. The book is fast-paced, so if you're unfamiliar with React and its friends, you'll need to pause along the way and do some research as the example application grows in features and dependencies. Along the way, Juntao points out some "smells" or signs that the approach can be improved – for example, cluttered code organization or hard-to-maintain test data.

Read this book if you would like to learn by example from someone who is an expert in using TDD to grow browser applications.

Evan Bottcher

March 2021

Foreword 2

Landing in the middle of a React project that had very low test coverage, in a team that had aspirations to improve it, but without a clear strategy of how to go about it, I struggled to find resources that stepped out how to approach testing for a front-end project. I couldn't find a clear explanation of how to implement Test-Driven Development for a UI, let alone specifically for React. This book couldn't have come at a better time.

There are a plethora of different testing methodologies and libraries available just for React. The ones you choose will depend on many things. This book doesn't prescribe a particular solution but establishes the purpose of tests in driving out specifications and suggests an overall approach, with practical guidance and examples. Juntao provides a holistic explanation of the purpose and implementation of Test-Driven Development for React, demonstrating the benefits of moving testing earlier in the process, improving the robustness and design of our code.

Juntao's years of experience, his eagerness and passion for learning and sharing his knowledge in a didactic way, help to make this a relevant, practical, and engaging guide to follow and have given me confidence in my own testing strategies.

Hannah Bourke
March 2021

Acknowledgments

When I first shared the news of this book to my ThoughtWorks colleagues, I got plenty of valuable feedback – from typos, grammar issues, to technical suggestions.

On a cool May morning of 2020, I received an email from Hannah Bourke; she said she liked the book and would like to give me some editing suggestions as a native English speaker and a developer. Then she started to send pull requests to the book's repository – they turned out to be not only good-quality language corrections but also many technical review comments from a learner's perspective.

Also, when I had the draft of the book, I invited several senior developers/writers at ThoughtWorks to review it. And after a while, I received some detailed comments from Martin Fowler; it was totally a surprise. As a developer and a famous writer, Martin taught me many things through these comments – it's really a long list – although the content of the book had changed since I sent out the draft, most of them are still valid and invaluable.

As he suggested, I've reduced almost one fourth of the content and tried to make the outline more clear and readable. Also, I trimmed off a bunch of not too relevant code snippets from examples and added more context setup before or after code. The most important lesson I learned from him is *simplicity* – try not to touch every aspect but focus on one topic at a time and discuss it deeply.

Introduction

Who Should Read This Book?

If you're a serious web application developer who wants to learn how to write high-quality code even under delivery pressure (with a tight deadline normally), it's the book just for you.

I'm expecting you have a passion for

- Learning a smooth and effective way to launch a new web application

- Learning how to apply TDD in your daily work

- Refactoring skills

- Improving code quality with more confidence

- Different schools of TDD

I assume that you have the basic understanding of how the elementary things like HTML, CSS, and JavaScript work in browsers. You don't have to be an expert, but you need to at least know how to write a basic HTML page from scratch with some css styles.

Also, you need to know basic concepts in JavaScript; some prior experience about any other programming language could help too.

How to Use This Book?

It's a practical book that requires a lot of hands-on work. To make the most of it, I think just reading it through would not be enough; you need to follow the steps in different chapters and try to do it yourself.

For the sake of simplicity, in most cases, I just put the "diff" or necessary snippets to demonstrate different concepts. If you want the full codebase for any reason, you can download it from this repo: `https://github.com/abruzzi/bookish-react-2nd`.

Juntao Qiu
September 2019
Melbourne

CHAPTER 1

A Very Brief History of Test-Driven Development

My intention in writing this chapter is not to copy and paste clichés from blogs (the following excerpt aside) or pretend I was part of the historic events (like the agile manifesto or Extreme Programming activities) that led to the creation of Test-Driven Development as a methodology – trust me, I'm not that old.

But I do think that giving you some context around what we're going to discuss in this book is beneficial. I'm going to talk about the basic workflow of Test-Driven Development (TDD) and different schools of doing it practically. If you want to jump into the code directly, feel free to do so and navigate to the next chapter to get your hands dirty.

Test-Driven Development

TDD is a software development methodology in which tests are written to drive the development of an application. It was developed/rediscovered by Kent Beck in the late 1990s as part of Extreme Programming and was well discussed in his famous book *Test-Driven Development: By Example*.

In his book, Kent Beck describes two essential rules:

- Write new code only if you first have a failing automated test
- Eliminate duplication

which leads to the steps of red-green-refactor, which we will discuss soon. The ultimate goal for these two rules is to write (as Ron Jeffries describes) clean code that works.

© Juntao Qiu 2021
J. Qiu, *Test-Driven Development with React*, https://doi.org/10.1007/978-1-4842-6972-5_1

Red-Green-Refactor Cycle

There is a well-known diagram that explains how to apply TDD practically – it's known as the red-green-refactor cycle (Figure 1-1).

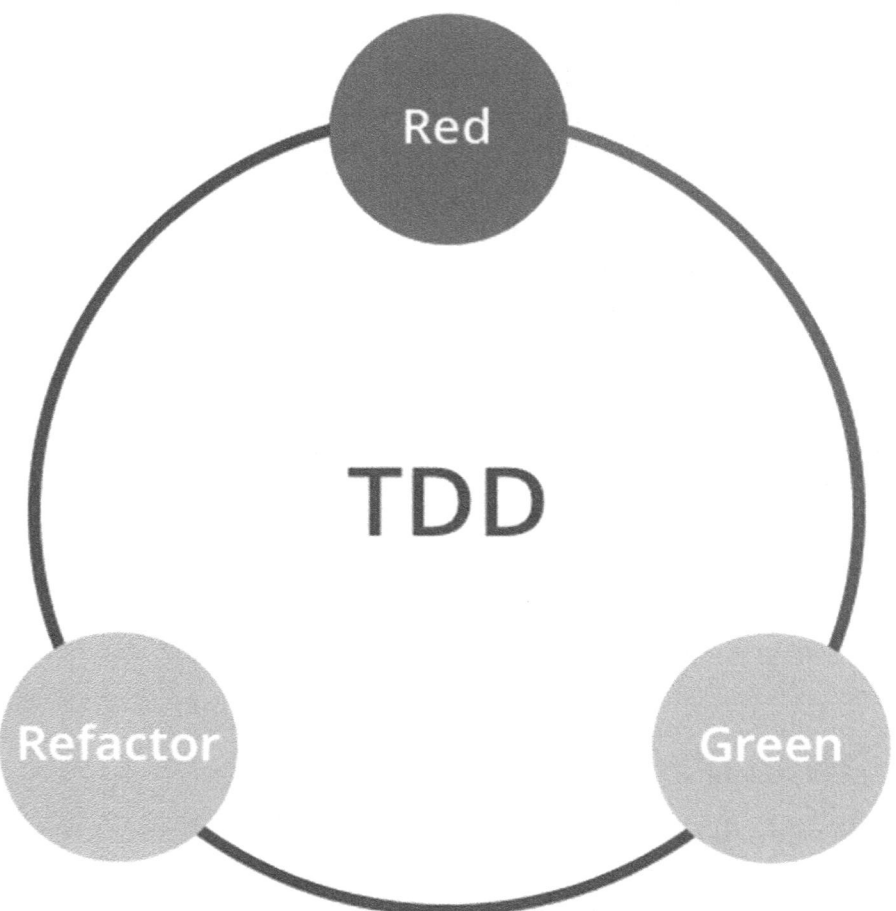

Figure 1-1. *Test-Driven Development*

Usually, there is a short description provided with this diagram, articulated as the three principles of TDD:

- Write a test and see it fail.

- Write just enough code to make the test pass.

- Refactor if any code smells are detected.

At first glance, it's pretty easy to follow. The problem here – as with many principles – is that they don't work well for beginners. The principles are quite high level and hard to apply because they lack detail. For example, just knowing the principles will not help you to answer questions like

- How can I write my very first test?

- What does enough code actually mean?

- When and how should I refactor?

A Closer Look at Red-Green-Refactor

Figure 1-2 takes a closer look at the process.

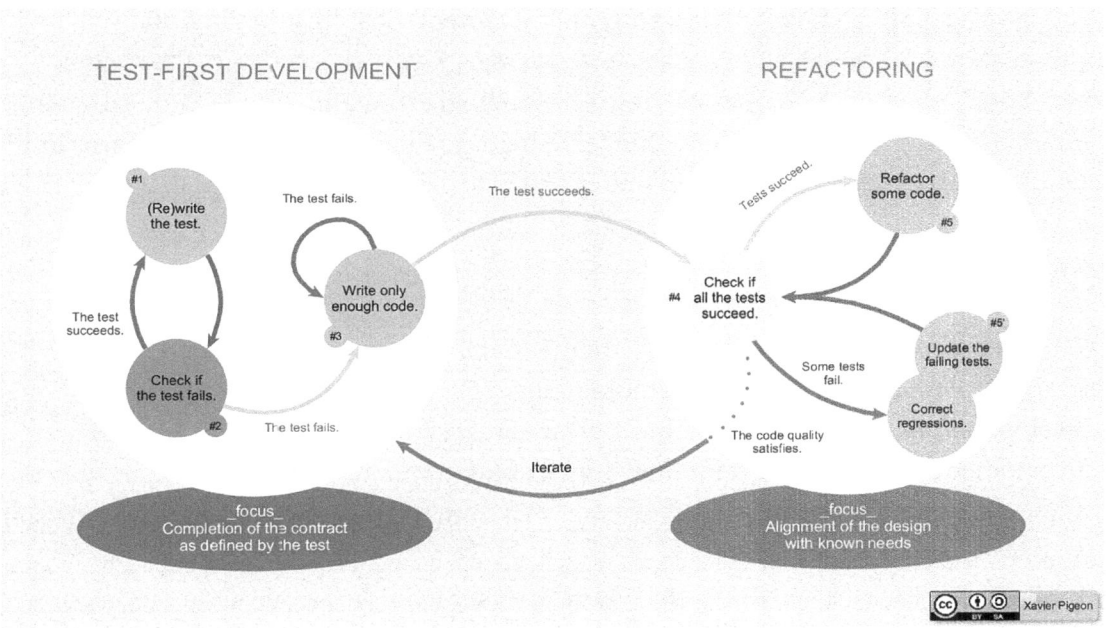

Figure 1-2. *Test-Driven Development. Source: Wikipedia (*`https://`
`en.wikipedia.org/wiki/Test-driven_development`*)*

Traditionally, TDD contains two parts: quick implementation and refactoring. In practice, the tests for quick implementation are not limited to the unit tests. They can be the acceptance tests as well – these are higher-level tests that focus more on business value and the end-user journey, without worrying too much about the technical details. Implementing the acceptance tests first could be an even better idea.

Starting with acceptance tests ensures that the right things are prioritized, and it provides confidence to developers when they want to clean up and refactor the code in the later stage. Acceptance tests are intended to be written from the end user's perspective; a passing acceptance test ensures the code meets the business requirement. Additionally, it can protect the developer from wasting time on false assumptions or invalid requirements.

There is a principle in Extreme Programming known as YAGNI, or you aren't gonna need it. YAGNI can be very useful for protecting developers from wasting their valuable time. Developers are very good at making assumptions around potential requirement changes, and based on those assumptions, they may come up with some unnecessary abstractions or optimizations that can make the code more generic or reusable. The problem is that those assumptions rarely turn out to be true. YAGNI emphasizes that you should not do it until you have to.

However, in the refactor phase, you can implement those abstractions and optimizations. Since you already have test coverage, it's much safer to do the cleanup then. Small refactors such as modifying a class name, extracting a method, or extracting some classes to a higher level – anything that helps to make the code more generic and SOLID – are now safer and easier to undertake.

Types of TDD

TDD is a big yet mixed concept. It has many variations and different schools, such as UTDD, BDD, ATDD, and so on. Traditionally, TDD implied Unit Test-Driven Development or UTDD. However, the TDD we are discussing in this book is ATDD (Acceptance Test-Driven Development), an extended version of the traditional concept, with an emphasis on writing the acceptance test from the business perspective and using it to drive out production code.

Having various tests in different layers can ensure that we are always on the right track and have the correct functionality.

Acceptance Test-Driven Development

In short, ATDD describes the behavior of the software from the end **user's point of view,** focusing on the business value of the application, rather than implementation **details.** Instead of verifying functions being called at certain times with correct **parameters, it** makes sure that when a user places an order, they receive their delivery **on time.**

We can merge the ATDD and UTDD into one diagram, as shown in Figure 1-3.

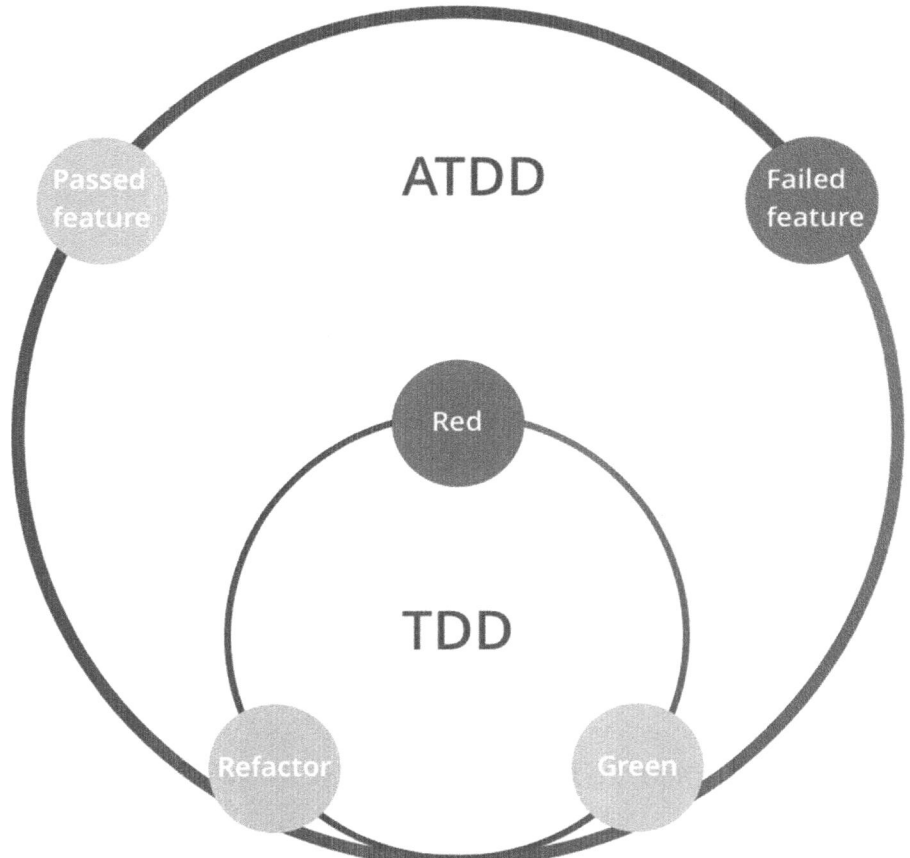

Figure 1-3. *Acceptance Test-Driven Development*

The diagram describes the following steps:

1. Write an acceptance test and see it fail.

2. Write a unit test and see it fail.

3. Write code to make the unit test pass.

4. Refactor the code.

5. Repeat 2–4, until acceptance test passes.

When you look at this process closely, you find that during the development stage, the acceptance test could be failing for quite some time. The feedback loop turns out to be very long, and there is a risk that an always-failed test means no test (protection) at all. Developers could be confused about whether there are defects in the implementation, or whether there is any implementation at all.

To resolve this problem, you have to write acceptance tests in relatively small chunks, testing a tiny slice of the requirement at a time. Alternatively, you could use the fake it until you make it approach, as we are going to use across this book.

The steps remain the same; only an extra fake step is added:

1. Write a failed acceptance test.

2. Make it pass in the most straightforward way (a fake implementation).

3. Refactor based on any code smells (like hard-coded data, magic number, etc.).

4. Add a new test based on new requirement (if we need a new acceptance test, go back to step 1; otherwise, the process is just like traditional TDD).

Note that in the second step, you can use hard-coding or a snippet of static HTML to make the test pass. At first glance, that may look redundant, but you will see the power of fake in the next few chapters.

The benefit of this variation is that when a developer is refactoring, there is always a passing acceptance test protecting you from breaking existing business logic. The drawback of this approach is that when a developer doesn't have enough experience, it can be difficult for them to come up with clean code designs – they could keep the fake in some way (e.g., a magic number, lack of abstractions, etc.).

Behavior-Driven Development

Behavior-Driven Development is an agile practice that encourages collaboration among different roles, developers, quality engineers, business analysts, or even other interested parties in a software project.

Although BDD is to some extent a general idea about how software development should be managed by both business interests and technical insight, the practice of BDD involves some specialized tools. For example, domain-specific language (DSL) is used to write tests in natural language that can be easily understood by nontechnical people and can be interpreted by code and executed behind the scenes.

For example, Listing 1-1 shows how a requirement can be described.

Listing 1-1. An example of BDD test case

```
Given there are `10` books in the library
When a user visits the homepage
Then they would see `10` books on the page
And each book would contain at least `name`, `author`, `price` and `rating`
```

Prerequisites of TDD

TDD has a strict and crucial prerequisite for developers: how to detect code smells and how to refactor them toward good design. For example, when you find some smelly code (e.g., lack of abstractions or magic numbers) and aren't sure how to make it better, then TDD alone cannot help you. Even though you are forced to use the orthodox workflow of TDD, you could end up with some unmaintainable tests in addition to poor-quality code.

Aware of Code Smell and Refactoring

In his book *Refactoring: Improving the Design of Existing Code*, Martin Fowler listed 68 refactorings. I would recommend this book as almost a mandatory prerequisite for anyone who values clean code and high-quality code. But don't worry too much; some of the refactorings he mentioned you may have already used in your daily work.

As mentioned earlier, a typical TDD workflow has three steps:

- A test case description requirement (specification).

- Some code to make the test pass.

- Refactor the implementation and tests.

A common misunderstanding is that test code is second tier or doesn't necessarily have the same importance as production code. I would argue that it is just as important as production code. Maintainable tests are crucial to people who have to make changes later on or add new ones. Every time you refactor, make sure the changes made in the production code are reflected in the test code.

Test First or Test Last

The hardest part of applying TDD in your daily workflow is that you have to write tests before you start writing any production code. For most developers, that's not just different and counterintuitive, but also breaks their own way of working significantly.

Nevertheless, the key to applying TDD is that you should build the fast feedback mechanism first. Once you have it, it doesn't matter much if you write the test first or last. By fast feedback, I mean that a method or an if-else branch can be tested in a very lightweight and effortless manner. If you add tests after all the functionality has been completed, you are not doing TDD by any means. Because you are missing the essential fast feedback loop – seen as the most important thing in development – you may also be missing the benefits promised by TDD.

By implementing a fast feedback loop, TDD ensures you are always on the right track – safely. It also gives you sufficient confidence to do the further code cleanup. And proper code cleanup can lead to a better code design. Of course, the cleanup does not come automatically; it requires extra time and effort. However, TDD is a great mechanism to protect you from breaking the whole application when you make any changes.

Techniques That Can Help Implement TDD

For the beginner, it can be challenging when applying TDD as it sometimes feels counterintuitive to test first. In practice, there are common reasons for resistance to TDD:

- For simple tasks, they don't need TDD.

- For complicated tasks, setting up the TDD mechanism itself can be too difficult.

There are a lot of tutorials and articles out there to describe techniques you should use to do TDD, and some may even involve describing how to split tasks before implementing TDD. However, things discussed in those tutorials are often oversimplified and can be hard to apply to a real-world project directly. For example, in a web application, both the interaction and a considerable portion of business logic now exist in the front end: the UI. The traditional techniques of how to write a unit test to drive back-end logic is already outdated.

Tasking

Another critical skill required by TDD is splitting a large requirement into smaller chunks through tasking. I would suggest every developer should learn how to split requirements before they even start to write their first test.

There is a classic joke: "how many steps to put an elephant into a fridge?" The answer is three steps:

- Open the fridge.

- Put the elephant in.

- Close it.

When we pick up a task, when we start to think through or discuss all the details, we may soon find we're trapped by a mountain of technical details and do not know where to start with. Our brain loves explicit and concrete things and hates abstraction – things that are invisible or implicit.

By utilizing some simple tools, we can make the work much more digestible for our brains, and tasking is one of these tools. It can help us divide a big task into smaller ones, which we can then tick off one after another.

For splitting a relatively big task into smaller pieces, a widely used principle is INVEST.

Separation Principle – INVEST

The mnemonic INVEST stands for

- Independent

- Negotiable

- Valuable

- Estimable

- Small

- Testable

When splitting a large requirement into smaller tasks, you need to ensure that each task fulfils those features. Firstly, for any given task, you should make it as independent as possible so it can be picked up and done in parallel along with others. Negotiable means it should not be fixed as a contract, and the scope of the task could change based on the trade-off of time and cost. For valuable, each task must provide some business value; the effort to make it should be measurable or has an estimation. Small means a task should be relatively small – a big piece means more unknown features and potentially would make the estimation less accurate. Finally, testable makes sure we know how the done looks like by verifying some key checkpoints.

For instance, when we want to develop a search function for an e-commerce system, we can use the INVEST principle to guide us through the analysis. Searching could be split as a few stories or tasks:

- A user can search products by name.

- A user can search products by branding.

- A user can search products by name and branding.

For user can search products by the name, we can keep using **INVEST** to split one story into a few tasks from a developer's perspective:

- Maintain the search result in memory (ArrayList + Java Stream API).

- Case-sensitive support.

- Wildcard (regular expression) support.

We can even keep using the same principle to split each item further:

- Write an acceptance test.

- Write code to make the test pass.

- Refactor.

- Write a unit test.

- Write code to make the test pass.

- Refactor.

- And so on.

That would lead us to a well-defined task to hand on and would allow us to verify each step clearly.

To-Do list with Post-it

Usually, we can stop at the second round of splitting, since the red-green-refactor is far too detailed in terms of tasking. And too granular tasks means more management effort (tracking those tasks needs more energy). To make the tasks visible, we can put it down on a post-it note and mark a simple tick once it's done (Figure 1-4).

By using this simple tool, you can then focus on what you're going to do and make the progress more accurate when you want to update it to other team members (e.g., in the daily stand-up meeting). By saying a task is 50% done, half of the items on the list are ticked off on the list you made earlier.

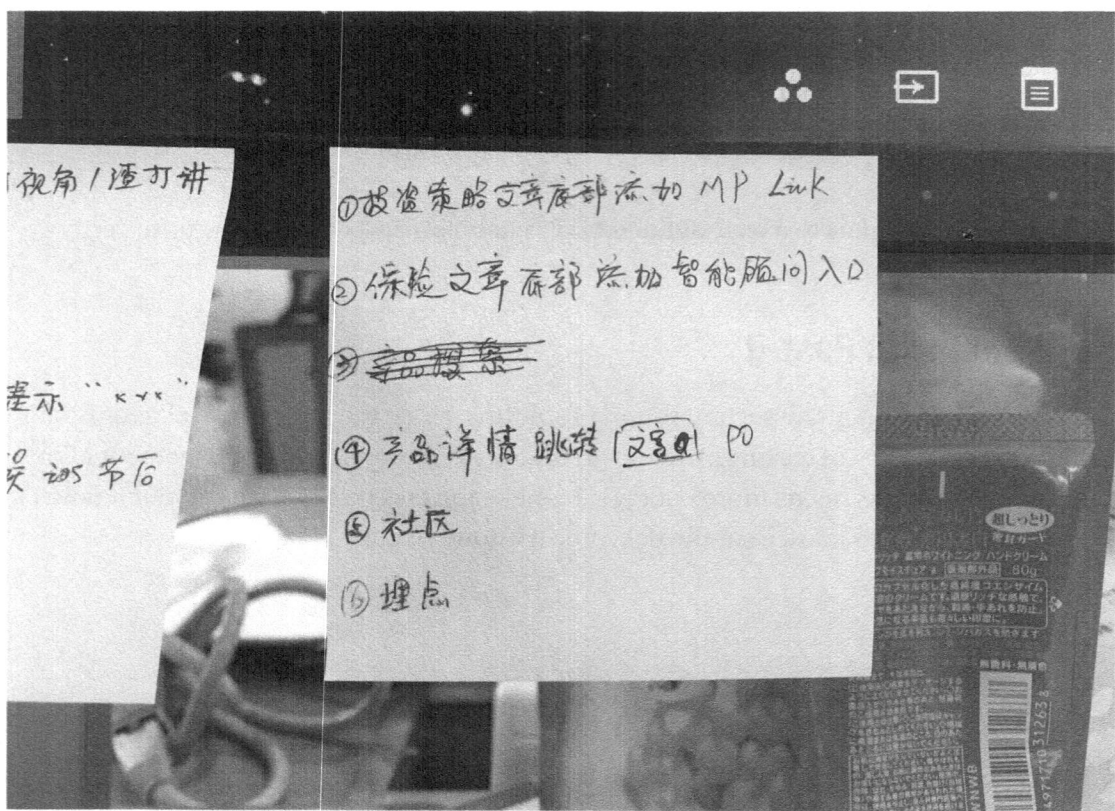

Figure 1-4. *Tasking*

Summary

We walked through the test pyramid and agile testing quadrants and introduced Acceptance Test-Driven Development as the way we write code through this book. When doing ATDD, we'll keep doing the classic red-green-refactor loop.

Refactoring depends on the sense and experience of identifying code smells. Once you find a code smell, you can then apply the corresponding refactoring technique. And then we may achieve maintainable, human-readable, extendable, and clean code along the way.

TDD always goes along with another powerful practice – tasking. You can use the INVEST principle to help you split a big task into smaller pieces. After the proper splitting, you can gradually improve the basic version and finish the big task iteratively.

In next chapter, we will introduce a concrete example to demonstrate how to apply TDD step by step. Along with that example, we will also cover the fundamental skills needed for implementing TDD, including how to use the jest testing framework and how to do tasking with real-world examples.

Further Reading

There is extensive debate around TDD – every now and then, you will see people are arguing about whether we need TDD or not or the right way to implement TDD. I found the following articles are really helpful in understanding some of those arguments:

- Uncle Bob has a great article discussing `test-first` or `test-last` approaches. If you haven't read it yet, I highly recommend you do.

- The latest and most famous debate regarding TDD came from `David Heinemeier Hansson (DHH)` (author of *Ruby on Rails*), `Kent Beck,` and `Martin Fowler`; you can find more here.

Also I highly recommend reading these books to build a solid foundation for implementing TDD. Even if you decided not to utilize TDD, those books are still highly recommended.

- *Clean Code: A Handbook of Agile Software Craftsmanship* by Robert C. Martin

- *Refactoring: Improving the Design of Existing Code* by Martin Fowler

CHAPTER 2

Get Started with Jest

In this chapter, we're going to learn some concepts and features about jest – a JavaScript testing framework – such as different types of matchers, the powerful and flexible expect, the extremely useful mock for unit testing, and so on. Additionally, we will learn how to arrange our test suite in an easy-to-maintain manner and leverage the best practices from real-world projects.

Firstly, you will see how to set up your environment to write our first test. We will be using ES6 as the primary programming language throughout this book.

So, without further ado, let's get started.

Set Up the Environment
Install Node.js

We're going to utilize node.js as the platform in this book for almost all scenarios. If you don't already have node installed on your computer, you can simply run the following command to install it on a MacOS with homebrew:

```
brew install node
```

Alternatively, if you are running a different operating system, or just want another option, node can be downloaded here.

Once you have it installed locally, you can then use npm (Node Package Manager) to install node packages – it's a binary program shipped with the node runtime.

Install and Config Jest

Jest is a testing framework from Facebook that allows developers to write reliable and fast running tests in a more readable syntax. It can watch changes in test/source files and rerun the necessary tests automatically. This allows you to get quick feedback,

15

© Juntao Qiu 2021
J. Qiu, *Test-Driven Development with React*, https://doi.org/10.1007/978-1-4842-6972-5_2

and that is a crucial factor in TDD. The speed of feedback can even determine whether TDD works for you or not. Simply put, the faster tests can run, the more efficient developers can be.

Let's firstly create a folder for our experiment and initialize the folder with a package.json to maintain all the following package installations:

```
mkdir jest-101
cd jest-101
npm init -y # init the current folder with default settings
```

Install jest as a development dependency, as we don't want to include jest into production package:

```
npm install --save-dev jest
```

After the installation, you can run jest --init to specify some default settings, such as where jest should find the test files and the source code, which environment (there are a lot) jest should run against (browser or node for the back end), and so on. You have to answer some questions to let jest understand your requirements; for now, let's just accept all the default settings by saying Yes to all the questions.

Note that if you have installed jest globally (with npm install jest -g), you can use the following command to init the config directly:

```
jest --init
```

Otherwise, you will have to use the local installation by npx, which looks for jest binary from node_modules/.bin/ and invokes it:

```
npx jest --init
```

For the sake of simplicity, we use node as test environment, without coverage report, and all other default settings like so:

```
npx jest --init
```

```
The following questions will help Jest to create a suitable configuration
for your project:

✓ Choose the test environment that will be used for testing › node
✓ Do you want Jest to add coverage reports? ... no
```

✓ Which provider should be used to instrument code for coverage? › v8
✓ Automatically clear mock calls and instances between every test? ... no

🏗 Configuration file created at /Users/juntaoqiu/learn/jest-101/jest.
config.js

Jest at First Glance

Cool, we're ready to write some tests to verify that all parts can work together now. Let's create a folder named src and put two files in calc.test.js and calc.js.

The file ends with *.test.js which means it's a pattern that jest will recognize and treat them as tests, as defined in the jest.config.js we generated previously:

```
//The glob patterns Jest uses to detect test files
testMatch: [
  "**/__tests__/**/*.js?(x)",
  "**/?(*.)+(spec|test).js?(x)"
],
```

Now, let's put some code in the calc.test.js:

```
var add = require('./calc.js')

describe('calculator', function() {
  it('add two numbers', function() {
    expect(add(1, 2)).toEqual(3)
  })
})
```

Here is something new if you never tried to write a test in jasmine (a very popular testing framework before jest era): the functions describe and it are inherited from jasmine. describe is a function that can be used to create a test suite, and you can define test cases (by using the it function) within it. It's the correct way to put human-readable text as the first parameter and the executable callback function as the second. For function it on the other hand, you can write the actual testing code.

The actual assertion is the statement expect(add(1, 2)).toEqual(3), which states that we're expecting the function call add(1, 2) to equal to 3.

add is imported from another file and is implemented like this:

```
function add(x, y) {
    return x + y;
}

module.exports = add
```

Then let's run the test and see how it goes:

```
npx jest
```

Alternatively, you can run the tests via

```
npm test
```

which invokes node_modules/.bin/jest under the hood, as shown in Figure 2-1.

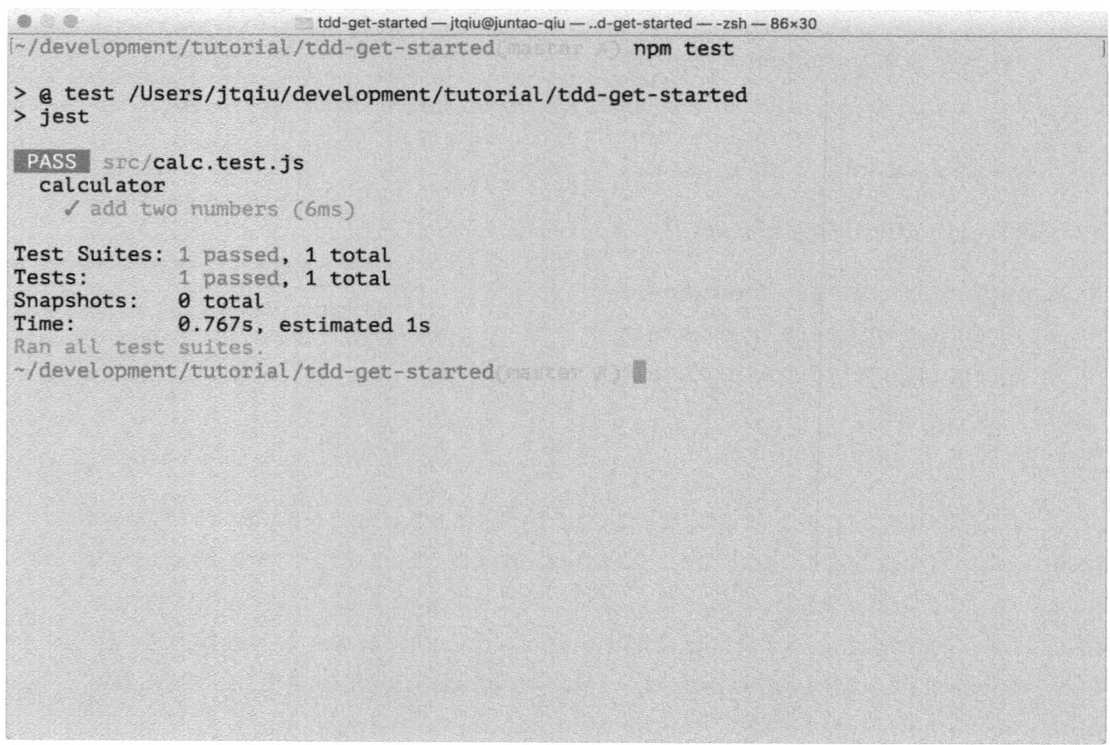

Figure 2-1. *First test*

Great, we have the very first test up and running.

Basic Concepts in Jest

In this section, we're about to go through some basic concepts in Jest. We use describe to define a test block. We can use that mechanism to arrange different test cases and gather relevant test cases together as a group.

Jest API: Describe and It

For example, we can put all arithmetic into one group:

```
describe('calculator', () => {
  it('should perform addition', () => {})
  it('should perform subtraction', () => {})
  it('should perform multiplication', () => {})
  it('should perform division', () => {})
})
```

What's more, we can next describe functions like so:

```
describe('calculator', () => {
  describe('should perform addition', () => {
    it('adds two positive numbers', () => {})
    it('adds two negative numbers', () => {})
    it('adds one positive and one negative numbers', () => {})
  })
})
```

The basic idea is to ensure relevant tests are grouped together so that the test description makes more sense for the people who maintain them. It's even more helpful if you can describe the description (the first parameter for function describe and it) within the business context, by using domain language.

Organize Your Tests Maintainer Friendly

For instance, when you are developing a hotel reservation application, the tests read like this:

```
describe('Hotel Sunshine', () => {
  describe('Reservation', () => {
    it('should make a reservation when there are enough rooms available',
    () => {})
```

```
    it('should warn the administrator when there are only 5 available rooms
    left', () => {})
  })

  describe('Checkout', () => {
    it('should check if any appliance is broken', () => {})
    it('should refund guest when checkout is earlier than planned',
    () => {})
  })
})
```

You may occasionally find some duplicated code scattered in test cases, for example, setting up a subject in each test is not uncommon:

```
describe('addition', () => {
  it('adds two positive numbers', () => {
    const options = {
      precision: 2
    }

    const calc = new Calculator(options)
    const result = calc.add(1.333, 3.2)
    expect(result).toEqual(4.53)
  })

  it('adds two negative numbers', () => {
    const options = {
      precision: 2
    }

    const calc = new Calculator(options)
    const result = calc.add(-1.333, -3.2)
    expect(result).toEqual(-4.53)
  })
})
```

Set Up and Tear Down

To reduce the duplication, we can use the beforeEach function that jest provides to define some reusable object instances. It is invoked automatically before jest runs each test case. In our case, the calculator instance can be used in all the test cases within the same describe block:

```
describe('addition', () => {
  let calc = null

  beforeEach(() => {
    const options = {
      precision: 2
    }
    calc = new Calculator(options)
  })

  it('adds two positive numbers', () => {
    const result = calc.add(1.333, 3.2)
    expect(result).toEqual(4.53)
  })

  it('adds two negative numbers', () => {
    const result = calc.add(-1.333, -3.2)
    expect(result).toEqual(-4.53)
  })
})
```

Of course, you may be wondering if there is a counterpart function named afterEach or something in charge of the cleanup work: there is!

```
describe('database', () => {
  let db = null;

  beforeEach(() => {
    db.connect('localhost', '9999', 'user', 'pass')
  })
```

```
afterEach(() => {
  db.disconnect()
})
})
```

Here, we establish a database connection before each test case and shut it down afterward. In practice, you may want to add a function to roll back the database changes or other cleanups in afterEach step.

Additionally, if you want something to be set up before all the test cases start and tear down after all of them are finished, then beforeAll and afterAll are there to help:

```
beforeAll(() => {
  db.connect('localhost', '9999', 'user', 'pass')
})

afterAll(() => {
  db.disconnect()
})
```

Using ES6

By default, you can only use ES5 (a relatively old version of JavaScript) in node.js (interestingly, by the time I started to write this chapter, I cannot use most of the features in ES6 directly with node runtime by default). However, since we're already in 2021, ES6 should be the default programming language you should choose for your front-end projects. Good news is that you don't have to wait till all the browsers implement the specification; you can use babel to translate and compile the ES6 code into ES5.

Install and Config Babel

It's pretty easy to set up; just installing a few packages can make it work properly:

```
npm install --save-dev babel-jest babel-core regenerator-runtime @babel/
preset-env
```

After the installation, create a .babelrc in your project root with content like

```
{
    "presets": [
        "@babel/preset-env"
    ]
}
```

That's it! Now you should be able to write ES6 in your source and test code, and babel will do the rest:

```
import {add} from './calc'

describe('calculator', () => {
    it('adds two numbers', () => {
            expect(add(1, 2)).toEqual(3)
    })
})
```

and

```
const add = (x, y) => x + y
export {add}
```

It's more neat and concise with arrow functions and one-line anonymous functions (like the add function). Also, I prefer import and export as I find it more readable than the old modules.export convention.

All tests should pass when you rerun npm test.

Using Matchers in Jest

Jest provides numerous helper functions (matchers) for developers to use for assertions when writing tests. Those matchers can be used to assert various data types in different scenarios.

Let's take a look at some basic usages first and then move into some more advanced examples later on.

Equality

toEqual and toBe may be the most common matchers you will find and use in almost every test case. As the name implies, they are used to assert whether values are equal to each other (the actual value and the expected value).

For example, it can be used for string, number, or composite objects:

```
it('basic usage', () => {
  expect(1+1).toEqual(2)
  expect('Juntao').toEqual('Juntao')
  expect({ name: 'Juntao' }).toEqual({ name: 'Juntao' })
})
```

And for toBe

```
it('basic usage', () => {
  expect(1+1).toBe(2) // PASS
  expect('Juntao').toBe('Juntao') // PASS
  expect({ name: 'Juntao' }).toBe({ name: 'Juntao' }) //FAIL
})
```

The last test will fail. For primitives like strings, numbers, and booleans, you can use toBe to test the equality. While for Objects, internally jest uses Object.is to check, which is strict and compares objects by memory address. So if you want to make sure all the fields are matching, use toEqual.

.not Method for Opposite Matching

Jest also provides .not that you can use to assert the opposite value:

```
it('basic usage', () => {
  expect(1+2).not.toEqual(2)
})
```

Sometimes, you might not want an exact match. Say you want a string to be matching some particular pattern. Then you can use toMatch instead:

```
it('match regular expression', () => {
  expect('juntao').toMatch(/\w+/)
})
```

In fact, you can write any valid regular expression:

```
it('match numbers', () => {
  expect('185-3345-3343').toMatch(/^\d{3}-\d{4}-\d{4}$/)
  expect('1853-3345-3343').not.toMatch(/^\d{3}-\d{4}-\d{4}$/)
})
```

Jest makes it very easy to work with strings. However, you can use comparisons with numbers too:

```
it('compare numbers', () => {
  expect(1+2).toBeGreaterThan(2)
  expect(1+2).toBeGreaterThanOrEqual(2)

  expect(1+2).toBeLessThan(4)
  expect(1+2).toBeLessThanOrEqual(4)
})
```

Matchers for Array and Object

Jest also provides matchers for Array and Object.

toContainEqual and toContain

For instance, it's quite common to test if an element is contained in an Array:

```
const users = ['Juntao', 'Abruzzi', 'Alex']

it('match arrays', () => {
  expect(users).toContainEqual('Juntao')
  expect(users).toContain(users[0])
})
```

Note that there is a difference between toContain and toContainEqual. Basically, toContain checks if the item is in the list by strictly comparing elements using ===. On the other hand, toContainEqual just checks the value (not the memory address).

For example, if you want to check whether an object is in a list

```
it('object in array', () => {
  const users = [
    { name: 'Juntao' },
    { name: 'Alex' }
  ]
  expect(users).toContainEqual({ name: 'Juntao' }) // PASS
  expect(users).toContain({ name: 'Juntao' }) // FAIL
})
```

The second assertion would fail since it uses a more strict comparison. As an object is just a combination of other JavaScript primitives, we can use dot notation and test the existence of the field or use the earlier matchers for fields in an object.

```
it('match object', () => {
  const user = {
    name: 'Juntao',
    address: 'Xian, Shaanxi, China'
  }

  expect(user.name).toBeDefined()
  expect(user.age).not.toBeDefined()
})
```

The Powerful Function Expect

We have tasted the matcher a little bit in previous sections; let's take a look at another super weapon Jest provided: the expect.

There are a few useful helper functions attached to the expect object:

- expect.stringContaining

- expect.arrayContaining

- expect.objectContaining

By using those functions, you can define your own `matcher`. For example:

```
it('string contains', () => {
  const givenName = expect.stringContaining('Juntao')
  expect('Juntao Qiu').toEqual(givenName)
})
```

The variable `givenName` here is not a simple value; it's a new matcher and matches strings containing `Juntao`.

Similarly, you can use `arrayContaining` to check a subset of an array:

```
describe('array', () => {
  const users = ['Juntao', 'Abruzzi', 'Alex']

  it('array containing', () => {
    const userSet = expect.arrayContaining(['Juntao', 'Abruzzi'])
    expect(users).toEqual(userSet)
  })
})
```

It looks a bit strange at first glance, but once you understand it, that pattern would help you to build more complicated matchers.

For instance, say we retrieve some data from the back-end API, with a payload that looks like

```
const user = {
  name: 'Juntao Qiu',
  address: 'Xian, Shaanxi, China',
  projects: [
    { name: 'ThoughtWorks University' },
    { name: 'ThoughtWorks Core Business Beach'}
  ]
}
```

For whatever reason, in our test, we don't care about `address` at all. We do care if the name field contains `Juntao` and the `project.name` contains `ThoughtWorks`.

The Containing Family Functions

So let's define a matcher by using the stringContaining, arrayContaining, and objectContaining like so:

```
const matcher = expect.objectContaining({
  name: expect.stringContaining('Juntao'),
  projects: expect.arrayContaining([
    { name: expect.stringContaining('ThoughtWorks') }
  ])
})
```

This expression describes exactly what we expect, and we can then use toEqual to do the assertion:

```
expect(user).toEqual(matcher)
```

As you can see, this pattern is pretty powerful. Basically, you can define a matcher just as you would in natural language. It could even be used in a contract between front-end and back-end services.

Build Your Matchers

Jest also allows you to extend the expect object to define your own matchers. In that way, you can enhance the default matcher set and make the test code more readable.

Let's see a concrete example in this section. As you might know, jsonpath is a library that allows developers to play with a JavaScript object – similar to xpath in XML.

Example: jsonpath Matcher

Install jsonpath first if you haven't yet:

```
npm install jsonpath --save
```

And then use it like this:

```
import jsonpath from 'jsonpath'

const user = {
  name: 'Juntao Qiu',
  address: 'Xian, Shaanxi, China',
```

```
  projects: [
    { name: 'ThoughtWorks University' },
    { name: 'ThoughtWorks Core Business Beach'}
  ]
}
```

```
const result = jsonpath.query(user, '$.projects')
console.log(JSON.stringify(result))
```

And you will get the result:

```
[[{"name":"ThoughtWorks University"},{"name":"ThoughtWorks Core Business Beach"}]]
```

and query $.projects[0].name

```
const result = jsonpath.query(user, '$.projects[0].name')
```

would get

```
["ThoughtWorks University"]
```

The query would return an empty array ([ ]) if the path didn't match **anything**:

```
const result = jsonpath.query(user, '$.projects[0].address')
```

Extend the Expect Function

Let's define a matcher named toMatchJsonPath as an extension by using function expect.extend:

```
import jsonpath from 'jsonpath'

expect.extend({
  toMatchJsonPath(received, argument) {
    const result = jsonpath.query(received, argument)

    if (result.length > 0) {
      return {
        pass: true,
        message: () => 'matched'
      }
```

```
      } else {
        return {
          pass: false,
          message: () => `expected ${JSON.stringify(received)} to match
          jsonpath ${argument}`
        }
      }
    }
})
```

So internally, Jest would pass two parameters to the customizing matcher; the first one is the actual result – the one you passed to function expect(). The second one, on the other hand, is the expected value you passed to the matcher, which in our case toMatchJsonPath.

For the return value, it's a simple JavaScript object that contains pass, which is a boolean value that indicates whether the test passes or not, and a message field to describe the reason for the pass or fail, respectively.

Once defined, you can use it in your test just like any other built-in matchers:

```
describe('jsonpath', () => {
  it('matches jsonpath', () => {
    const user = {
      name: 'Juntao'
    }
    expect(user).toMatchJsonPath('$.name')
  })

  it('does not match jsonpath', () => {
    const user = {
      name: 'Juntao',
      address: 'ThoughtWorks'
    }
    expect(user).not.toMatchJsonPath('$.age')
  })
})
```

Pretty cool, right? It is sometimes very useful when you want to make the matcher more readable by using some domain-specific language.

For example:

```
const employee = {}
expect(employee).toHaveName('Juntao')
expect(employee).toBelongToDepartment('Product Halo')
```

Mock and Stub

In most cases, you just don't want to make the real call to underlying external functions in a unit test. You would like to mock it – just pretend that we're calling the real thing. For example, you might not want to send an email to the client when you just want to test the email template functionality. Instead, you would like to see whether the HTML generated contains correct content or you just verify it sends an email to a particular address. Aside from that, connecting to a product database to test the deletion API works would be not acceptable in most situations.

jest.fn for Spying

So we, as developers, need to set up a mechanism to enable this. Jest provides a variety of ways to do this mock. The simplest one is function jest.fn to set up a spy for a function:

```
it('create a callable function', () => {
  const mock = jest.fn()
  mock('Juntao')
  expect(mock).toHaveBeenCalled()
  expect(mock).toHaveBeenCalledWith('Juntao')
  expect(mock).toHaveBeenCalledTimes(1)
})
```

You can use jest.fn() to create a function that could be invoked just like other regular functions, except it provides the ability to be audited. A mock can track all the invocations to it. And it can record the invoke times and the parameter passed in for each invoke. That could be very useful, since in many scenarios, we just want to ensure the particular function has been called with specified parameters, and in the correct order – we don't have to do the real invocation.

Mock Implementation

A dummy mock object as seen in the previous example doesn't do anything interesting. The following one is more meaningful:

```
it('mock implementation', () => {
  const fakeAdd = jest.fn().mockImplementation((a, b) => 5)

  expect(fakeAdd(1, 1)).toBe(5)
  expect(fakeAdd).toHaveBeenCalledWith(1, 1)
})
```

Instead of defining a static mock, you can define an implementation by yourself too. The real implementation could be very complicated; maybe it does some calculation based on a complex formula on some given parameters.

Stub a Remote Service Call

Additionally, just imagine we have a function that invokes a remote API call to fetch data:

```
export const fetchUser = (id, process) => {
  return fetch(`http://localhost:4000/users/${id}`)
}
```

In the test code, especially in a unit test, we don't want to perform any remote calls, so we use mock instead. In this example, we're testing that our function fetchUser will call the global fetch:

```
describe('mock API call', () => {
  const user = {
    name: 'Juntao'
  }

  it('mock fetch', () => {
    // given
    global.fetch = jest.fn().mockImplementation(() => Promise.
    resolve({user}))
    const process = jest.fn()
```

```
// when
fetchUser(111).then(x => console.log(x))

// then
expect(global.fetch).toHaveBeenCalledWith('http://localhost:4000/
users/111')
  })
})
```

We expect that the `fetch` is invoked by `http://localhost:4000/users/111`; note the `id` we are using here. And we can see that the user information is printed out on the console:

```
PASS   src/advanced/matcher.test.js
  • Console

    console.log src/advanced/matcher.test.js:152
      { user: { name: 'Juntao' } }
```

That is something very useful. `Jest` provides other mock mechanisms as well, but we are not going to discuss them here. We are not using any advanced features in this book other than what we have addressed earlier.

If you are interested, please check `jest` help or homepage for more information.

Summary

We learned about how to set up ES6 and `jest` at the beginning of this chapter and then walked through some fundamental concepts of the `jest` test frameworks, as well as different types of `matchers` and how to use them. We defined a `jsonpath` matcher by ourselves and learned how it could simplify the matching process in our tests and make tests more concise and readable.

CHAPTER 3

Test-Driven Development 101

In this chapter, we will learn how to apply TDD in our daily development routine through a step-by-step guide. Along with this demo, you will get an idea of how to split a big task into relatively smaller ones and complete each one with a set of passing tests while learning some refactoring techniques. Before we dive into the code, let's get a fundamental understanding of how to write a proper test.

Writing Tests

So how would you start to write a test? Typically, there are three steps (as always, even to put an elephant into a fridge) required. Firstly, do some preparation work, like setting up the database, initializing the object to be tested, or loading some fixture data. Secondly, invoke the method or function to be tested, usually assigning the result to some variable. Finally, do some assertions to see whether the result is as expected or not.

Using Given-When-Then to Arrange a Test

It's usually described as Given, When, and Then or in the 3As format, where the As stands for Arrange, Act, and Assert. Both describe the same process.

In the Given clause, you describe all the preparation, including setting up dependencies. In When, you trigger the action or change the state of a subject to be tested, usually a function call with prepared parameters. Finally, in Then, you examine the result to see if it matches the expected result in some way (equals to something exactly, or contains particular patterns or throws an error, and so on).

© Juntao Qiu 2021
J. Qiu, *Test-Driven Development with React*, https://doi.org/10.1007/978-1-4842-6972-5_3

As an example, say we have the following snippet:

```
// given
const user = User.create({ name: 'Juntao', address: 'ThoughtWorks Software
Technologies (Melbourne)' })

// when
const name = user.getName()
const address = user.getAddress()

// then
expect(name).toEqual('Juntao')
expect(address).toEqual('ThoughtWorks Software Technologies (Melbourne)')
```

Typically, you will split test cases with many assertions into several independent ones and let each have a single assertion, like

```
it('creates user name', () => {
  // given
  const user = User.create({ name: 'Juntao', address: 'ThoughtWorks
Software Technologies (Melbourne)' })

  // when
  const name = user.getName()

  // then
  expect(name).toEqual('Juntao')
});

it('creates user address', () => {
  // given
  const user = User.create({ name: 'Juntao', address: 'ThoughtWorks
  Software Technologies (Melbourne)' })

  // when
  const address = user.getAddress()

  // then
  expect(address).toEqual('ThoughtWorks Software Technologies (Melbourne)')
});
```

Triangulation Method

There are a couple of ways to write tests and drive the implementation. One commonly accepted approach is called `triangulation`. Let's take a close look at how to do it with some examples.

Example: function `addition`

Imagine we are implementing a calculator with TDD. A test for `addition` could be a good starting point.

The First Test for `addition`

The specification of `addition` could be

```
describe('addition', () => {
  it('returns 5 when adding 2 and 3', () => {
    const a = 2, b = 3
    const result = add(a, b)
    expect(result).toEqual(5)
  })
})
```

A `Simple` Implementation

And the simplest implementation can be

```
const add = () => 5
```

   At first glance, it might seem very strange to write your function like this. But it has several benefits. For example, it's a good way for a developer to verify if everything is connected correctly. Just modify the value 5, showed earlier, to 3 to see if the test is failing or not. When test and implementation are not linked properly, you can get a misleading *green* test.

The Second Test Case to Make Our Implementation Less Specific

We can create another test for our add function:

```
it('returns 6 when adding 2 and 4', () => {
    const a = 2, b = 4
    const result = add(a, b)
    expect(result).toEqual(6)
})
```

To make the test pass, the simplest solution then becomes

```
const add = (a, b) => 2 + b
```

The idea is to write a failing but specific test to drive the implementation code to be more generic, in each step. So now, the implementation is more generic than in the first step. However, there's still some room for improvement.

The Final and Simple Implementation

The third test could be something like

```
it('returns 7 when adding 3 and 4', () => {
    const a = 3, b = 4
    const result = add(a, b)
    expect(result).toEqual(7)
})
```

This time there are no patterns in the test data to follow, so we have to write something more complicated to make it pass. The implementation becomes

```
const add = (a, b) => a + b
```

Now the implementation is more generic and will cover most additional scenarios. In the future, our calculator might need to support `addition` for imaginary numbers; we can do that by adding more tests to drive out the solution in the same way.

This approach of writing tests is called `Triangulation`: you write a failed test and write just *enough* code to make the test pass, and then you write another test to drive the changes from another angle. And that, in turn, will lead you to make the implementation more generic. You continue working in this manner, step by step, until the code becomes generic enough to support most of the cases that fall within the business requirements.

At first glance, it might seem too simple and slow to be an effective way to write software, but it is a solid foundation you can and should rely on. For both simple tasks and more complicated ones, you apply the same process. This links back to a key part of TDD which is being able to simplify tasks and split bigger tasks into smaller pieces.

Ok, let's move one step further by looking into applying TDD in a more complicated example.

How to Implement Tasking with TDD

In the project I'm currently working on, our team uses a very simple manner to track the efforts put into each user story (a small chunk of work that could be accomplished independently). Usually, in a agile project each card or ticket can have one of the following statuses: analysis, doing, or testing, done as it progresses through its life cycle. It could also be blocked when something it depends on is incomplete or not yet ready.

The measure of efforts on stories we're using is pretty simple. Basically, we track how many days were spent on coding or how many days it was blocked. The project manager then has a chance to understand what progress looks like and what the overall health status of the project is and maybe any further actions that could be taken to improve it.

We put a d in lower case in the title of a card to indicate that it has been under development for half a day and an uppercase D for a full day. Not surprisingly, q for half a Quality Assurance day and Q for a whole QA day. This means that at any given moment, you will see something like this on the title of the card: [ddDQbq] Allow users to login to their profile page – the b is for blocked.

An Expression Parser for Tracking Progress

Let's build a parser that can read the tracking marks ddDQbq and translate it into a human-readable format, something like this:

```
{
  "Dev days": 2.0,
  "QA days": 1,
  "Blocked": 0.5
}
```

Looks pretty straightforward, right? Can't wait to jump in and write the code? Hold on, let's get started with a test first and get a feeling of how to apply TDD in such a case.

Spilt the Parser to Sub-tasks

So the first question could be: **how can we split a task like this into smaller tasks that are easy to achieve and verify?** While there are multiple ways to do it, a reasonable split could be

1. Write a test to make sure we can translate d to half dev day.

2. Write a test to make sure we can translate D to one dev day.

3. Write a test to handle more than one mark like dD.

4. Write a test to handle q.

5. Write a test to handle qQ.

6. Write a test to handle ddQ.

As we discussed in Chapter 1, the splitting is essential for applying TDD. And small tasks should be engaging and encourage you in different ways:

7. It's fun (it has been proven that when we experience small amounts of achievement, our brains release dopamine, which is connected to feelings of pleasure, learning, and motivation).

8. It ensures fast feedback.

9. It allows you to easily understand the progress of the task at any given time.

All right, once we have these steps defined, we're ready to implement them one by one with TDD.

Applying TDD Step by Step

As we already have the tasks split, we then only need to translate them into corresponding unit test. Let's start with our first test.

The First Test – Parse and Calculate Mark d

Ok, enough theory, let's get our hands dirty. According to the output of the tasking step, the first test should be

```
it('translates d to half a dev day', () => {
  expect(translate('d')).toEqual({'Dev': 0.5})
})
```

And pretty straightforwardly, the implementation could be as simple as

```
const translate = () => ({'Dev': 0.5})
```

It ignores the input and returns a dummy {'Dev': 0.5}, but you have to admire that it fulfils the requirement regarding the current sub-task. Quick and dirty, but it works.

The Second Test – For Mark D

Let's cross off the first to-do on our task list and move on:

```
it('translates D to one dev day', () => {
  expect(translate('D')).toEqual({'Dev': 1.0})
})
```

What's the most straightforward solution you can think of? Maybe something like this:

```
const translate = (c) => (c === 'd' ? {'Dev': 0.5}: {'Dev': 1.0})
```

I know it seems silly to write code in this way. However, as you can see, our implementation is driven by the related tests. As long as the tests pass – which means the requirements are met – we could call it satisfied. After all, the only reason we write code is to fulfil some business requirement, right?

As the tests are now passing, you can do some refactoring if you find something could be improved, for example, magic numbers, or the method body is too long. For now, I think we're ok to continue.

The Combination of Notes d and D

The third test could be

```
it('translates dD to one and a half dev days', () => {
  expect(translate('dD')).toEqual({'Dev': 1.5})
})
```

Hmm, things become more complicated now; we have to parse the string of characters individually and sum up the result. The following code snippet should do the trick:

```
const translate = (input) => {
  let sum = 0;
  input.split('').forEach((c) => sum += c === 'd' ? 0.5: 1.0)
  return {'Dev': sum}
}
```

Now our program can handle all the d or D combination sequences like ddd or DDdDd without a problem. Then comes task four:

```
it('translates q to half a qa day', () => {
  expect(translate('q')).toEqual({'QA': 0.5})
})
```

It seems we need a sum function for each status, for example, sum in Dev, sum in QA. It would be more convenient if we can refactor the code a little to make that change easier. And thus, the most beautiful part of TDD emerges – you don't have to worry about breaking any of the existing functionalities by accident since you have the tests to cover them.

Refactoring – Extract Functions

Let's extract the parsing part out as a function itself and use that function in translate. The translate function could then be something like this after the refactoring:

```
const parse = (c) => {
  switch(c) {
    case 'd': return {status: 'Dev', effort: 0.5}
    case 'D': return {status: 'Dev', effort: 1}
  }
}
```

```
const translate = (input) => {
  const state = {
    'Dev': 0,
    'QA': 0
  }

  input.split('').forEach((c) => {
    const {status, effort} = parse(c)
    state[status] = state[status] + effort
  })

  return state
}
```

Now it should be effortless to make the new test pass. We can add one new case in parse:

```
const parse = (c) => {
  switch(c) {
    case 'd': return {status: 'Dev', effort: 0.5}
    case 'D': return {status: 'Dev', effort: 1}
    case 'q': return {status: 'QA', effort: 0.5}
  }
}
```

Keep Refactoring – Extract Functions to Files

For the task that contains different characters, there is no change required in the code at all. However, as a responsible programmer, we could keep cleaning the code up to an *ideal* status. For example, we could extract the parse to a lookup dictionary:

```
const dict = {
  'd': {
    status: 'Dev',
    effort: 0.5
  },
```

```
  'D': {
    status: 'Dev',
    effort: 1.0
  },
  'q': {
    status: 'QA',
    effort: 0.5
  },
  'Q': {
    status: 'QA',
    effort: 1.0
  }
}
```

and that would simplify the parse function to something like

```
const parse = (c) => dict[c]
```

You can even extract the dict as data into a separate file named constants and import it into translator.js for the sake of clarity. For the forEach function in translate, we could use Array.reduce to make it even shorter:

```
const translate = (input) => {
  const items = input.split('')
  return items.reduce((accumulator, current) => {
    const { status, effort } = parse(current)
    accumulator[status] = (accumulator[status] || 0) + effort
    return accumulator
  }, {})
}
```

Nice and clean, right? As you can see in Figure 3-1, all the tests now are passing.

```
PASS  src/translator.test.js
translator
  ✓ translate d to half dev day (6ms)
  ✓ translate D to one dev day (1ms)
  ✓ translate dD to one and a half dev day (1ms)
  ✓ translate q to half qa day (1ms)
  ✓ translate qQ to one and a half qa day
  ✓ translate dddQ (1ms)
```

Figure 3-1. *All tests cases for translator are passing*

Note that the refactoring process can keep going until you feel comfortable with the code. Be careful not to over engineer it by putting too many assumptions around potential changes or abstracting the code to a level beyond what is helpful.

Summary

We learned the three basic steps for writing a proper test and now understand how to use Triangulation to drive out different paths in tests. We also learned how to perform tasking to help us to write tests. Next, we walked through a reasonably small program in the TDD fashion step by step and finally got something useful in a real-life scenario.

CHAPTER 4

Project Setup

Before we jump into the main content of this book, we need to set up several infrastructures. We will set up project codebase and skeleton code with `create-react-app` and install/config `Material-UI` framework to simplify the user interface development; last but not least, we will set up the end-to-end UI testing framework `Cypress`.

Application Requirements

In this book, we are going to develop a web application from scratch. We will call it `Bookish`; it's a simple application about `books` – as the name implies. In the application, a user could have a book list and can search books by keywords, and users are allowed to navigate to a book detail page and review the `description`, `review`, and `ranking` of the book. We will complete some of the features in an iterative manner, applying `ATDD` along the way.

In the application, we will develop several typical features including the book list and book detail pages, as well as the searching and reviewing functionalities.

Feature 1 – Booklist

In the real world, the granularity of a feature would be much bigger than the ones we're describing in this book. Typically, there would be many user stories within a feature, such as book list, pagination, the styling of the book list, and so on. Let's assume there is only one story per feature here.

- Show the booklist.

We can describe the user story in this form:

As a user I want to see a list of books So that I can learn something new

© Juntao Qiu 2021
J. Qiu, *Test-Driven Development with React*, https://doi.org/10.1007/978-1-4842-6972-5_4

This is a very popular format to describe a user story, and there are good reasons for that. By describing `As a <role>`, it stresses who would benefit from this feature, and by saying `I want to <do something>`, you're explaining how the user would interact with the system. Finally, `So that <value>` sentence describes the business value behind this feature.

This format forces us to think from the stakeholder's perspective and hopefully tell both business analysts and developers what the most important (valuable) point is of the user story they are working on.

The acceptance criteria are

- Given there are ten books in the system, a user should see ten items on the page.

- In each item, the following information should be displayed: book name, author, price, and rating.

Acceptance criteria can sometimes be written in the following manner:

```
Given there are `10` books in the library
When a user visits the homepage
Then he/she would see `10` books on the page
And each book would contain at least `name`, `author`, `price` and `rating`
```

The given clause explains the current status of the application, when it means the user triggers some action, for example, clicks a button or navigates to a page, and then is an assertion that states the expected performance of the application.

Feature 2 – Book Detail

- Show book detail.

As a user, I want to see the details of a book So that I can quickly get an understanding of what it's about.

And the acceptance criteria are

- User clicks an item in the book list and is redirected to the details page.

- The details page displays the book name, author, price, description, and any reviews.

Feature 3 – Searching

- Searching by book name

As a user, I want to search for a book by its name So that I can quickly find what I'm interested in.

And the acceptance criteria are

- The user types `Refactoring` as a search word.

- Only books with `Refactoring` in their name are displayed in the booklist.

Feature 4 – Reviews

- Besides the other information on the detail page

As a user, I want to be able to add a review to a book I have read previously So that people who have the same interests could decide if it is worthwhile to read.

And the corresponding acceptance criteria are

- A user can read the reviews on the detail page.

- A user can post a review to a particular book.

- A user can edit the review they have posted.

With all those requirements well defined, we can start with project setting up.

Create the Project

Let's get started with some essential package installation and configuration first. Make sure you have node (at least node >= 8.10 and npm >= 5.6 are required) installed locally. After that, you can use npm to install the tools we need to build our Bookish application (we have already covered that part in the previous chapter; check it out in case you haven't).

Using create-react-app

After the installation is complete, we can use the `create-react-app` package to create our project:

```
npx create-react-app bookish-react
```

create-react-app will install react, react-dom, and a command-line tool named react-scripts by default. Moreover, it will download those libraries and their dependencies automatically, including webpack, babel, and others. By using create-react-app, we don't need any config to get the application up and running.

After the creation process, as the console log suggests, we can jump into the bookish-react folder and run npm start, and then you should be able to see it launches like Figure 4-1:

```
cd bookish-react
npm start
```

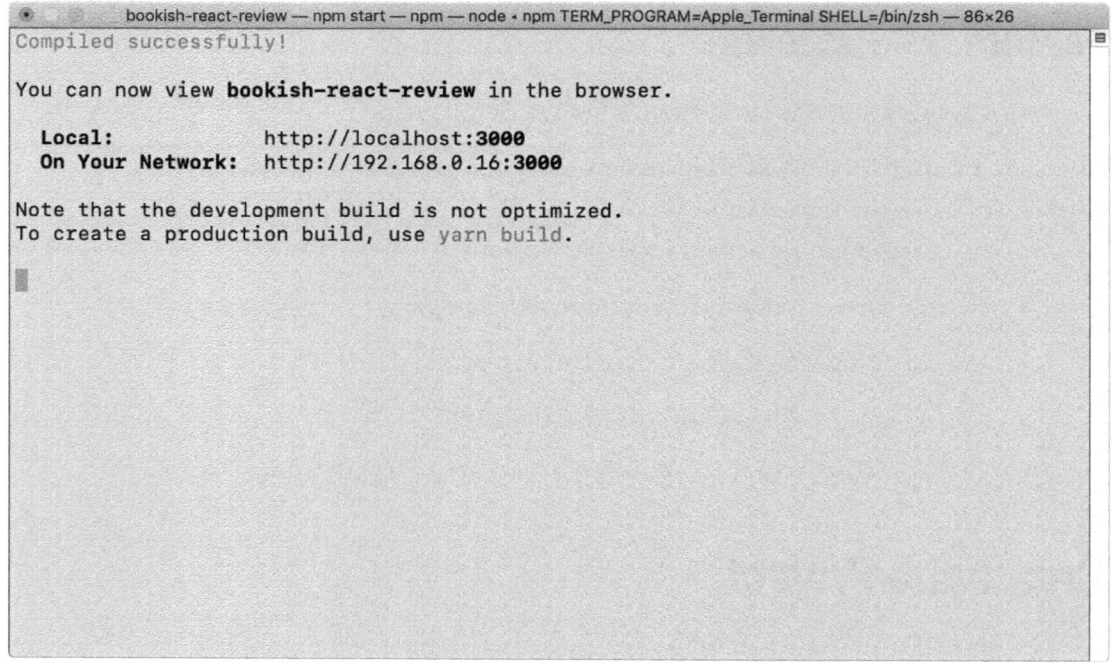

Figure 4-1. *Launch your application in terminal*

There will be a new browser tab opened automatically at this address: http://localhost:3000. And the UI should look like Figure 4-2.

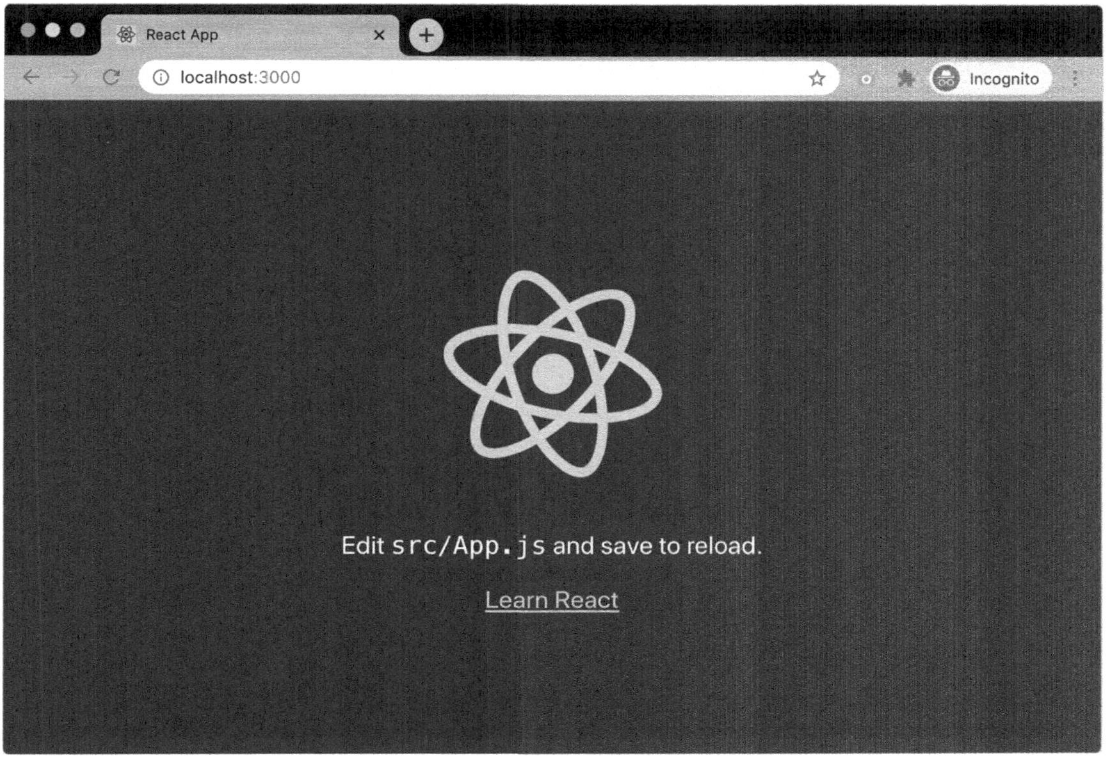

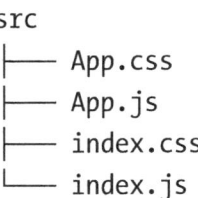

Figure 4-2. *The application running in browser*

Project File Structure

We don't need all of the files generated by `create-react-app`, so let's do some clean up first. We can remove all the irrelevant files in `src` folder, leaving us with the following files:

```
src
├── App.css
├── App.js
├── index.css
└── index.js
```

Modify the App.js file content so it looks as follows:

```
import React from 'react';
import './App.css';

function App() {
  return (
    <div className='App'>
      <h1>Hello world</h1>
    </div>
  );
}

export default App;
```

And the index.js like this:

```
import React from 'react';
import ReactDOM from 'react-dom';
import './index.css';
import App from './App';

ReactDOM.render(<App />, document.getElementById('root'));
```

Then our UI should look something like Figure 4-3.

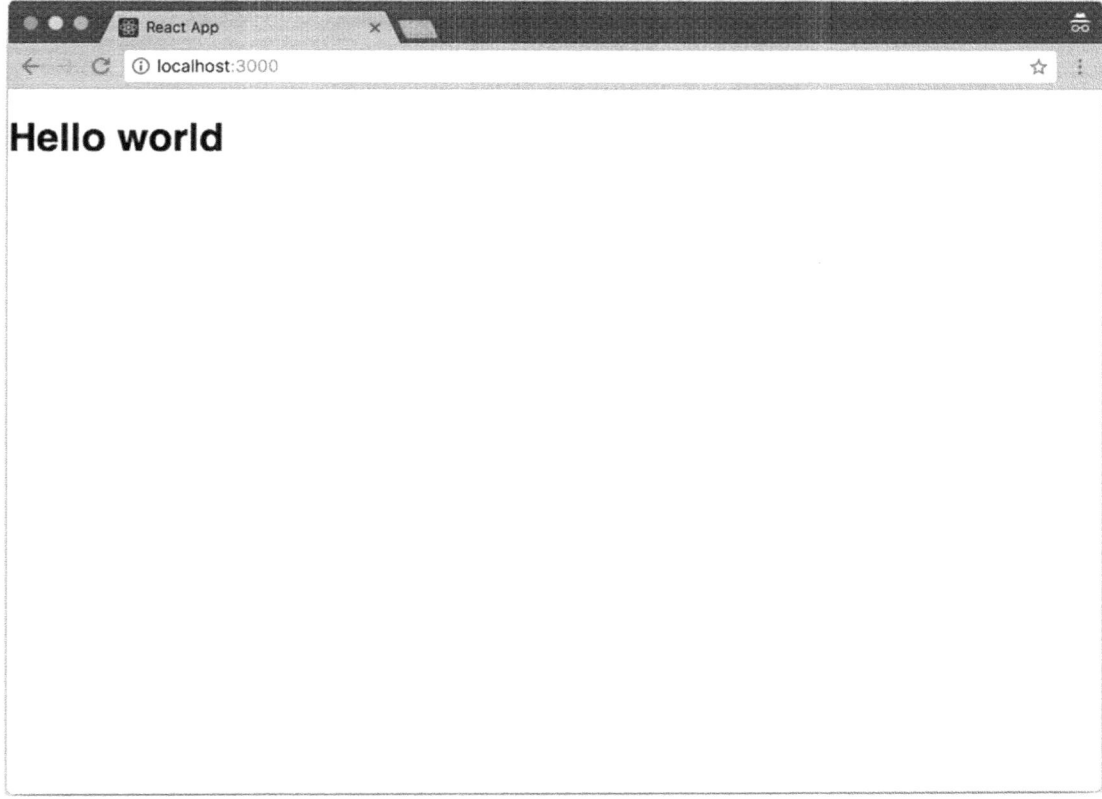

Figure 4-3. *After clean up*

Material-UI Library

To make the application we're demonstrating here look more realistic, as well as reduce the css tricks in the code snippets, we will use Material-UI. This library contains many reusable components that are ready to be used out of the box, such as Tabs, ExpandablePanel, and others. It will help us to build our bookish app faster and more easily.

The installation is pretty straightforward; another npm install will do:

```
npm install @material-ui/core @material-ui/icons --save
```

After that, let's put some fonts in our public/index.html to improve the look and feel.

Font and Icons

Note the second line is for svg icons:

```
<link rel='stylesheet' href='https://fonts.googleapis.com/css?family=Roboto
:300,400,500,700&display=swap' />
<link rel='stylesheet' href='https://fonts.googleapis.com/
icon?family=Material+Icons' />
```

That's all we need for now.

Using Typography as an Example

We can use a Component from material-ui in our code, importing the module like this in App.js:

```
import { Typography } from '@material-ui/core';
```

And then change the h1 to <Typography>:

```
<Typography variant='h2' component='h2' data-test='heading'>
Bookish
</Typography>
```

By using Material-UI, we don't need a separate file for css anymore, as it utilizes the css-in-js approach to make the component encapsulated and independent. We can then remove all the .css files, making sure to also remove any references to them.

Now, the project structure has just two files left:

```
src
├─── App.js
└─── index.js
```

index.js should look like this:

```
import React from 'react';
import ReactDOM from 'react-dom';

import App from './App';

ReactDOM.render(<App />, document.getElementById('root'));
```

and App.js like this:

```
import React from 'react';
import Typography from '@material-ui/core/Typography';

function App() {
  return (
    <div>
      <Typography variant='h2' component='h2' data-test='heading'>
      Bookish
      </Typography>
    </div>
  );
}

export default App;
```

Cypress

In the first edition of this book, I used puppeteer as the engine for UI functional tests, and it's a great tool for that purpose. However, I found its API is too low level from most beginners. From the end-user perspective, you have to remember a lot of unnecessary details such as async/await pairs when querying elements on the page. And it does not provide basic helpers, such as fixtures or stubs, which are widely used in TDD.

So this time, I will use Cypress instead – the idea is pretty much the same, Cypress gives us more options and better mechanisms to reduce the effort of writing tests. Features such as fixture and route are shipped with the tool that can make our life much easier.

The good news is that installation is simple, and you don't have to configure it at all.

Setting Up Cypress

Let's run the following command to start:

```
npm install cypress --save-dev
```

After the installation, make sure the app is running, and then we can run the `cypress` command to launch the GUI to create our first test suite as seen in Figure 4-4:

```
npx cypress open
```

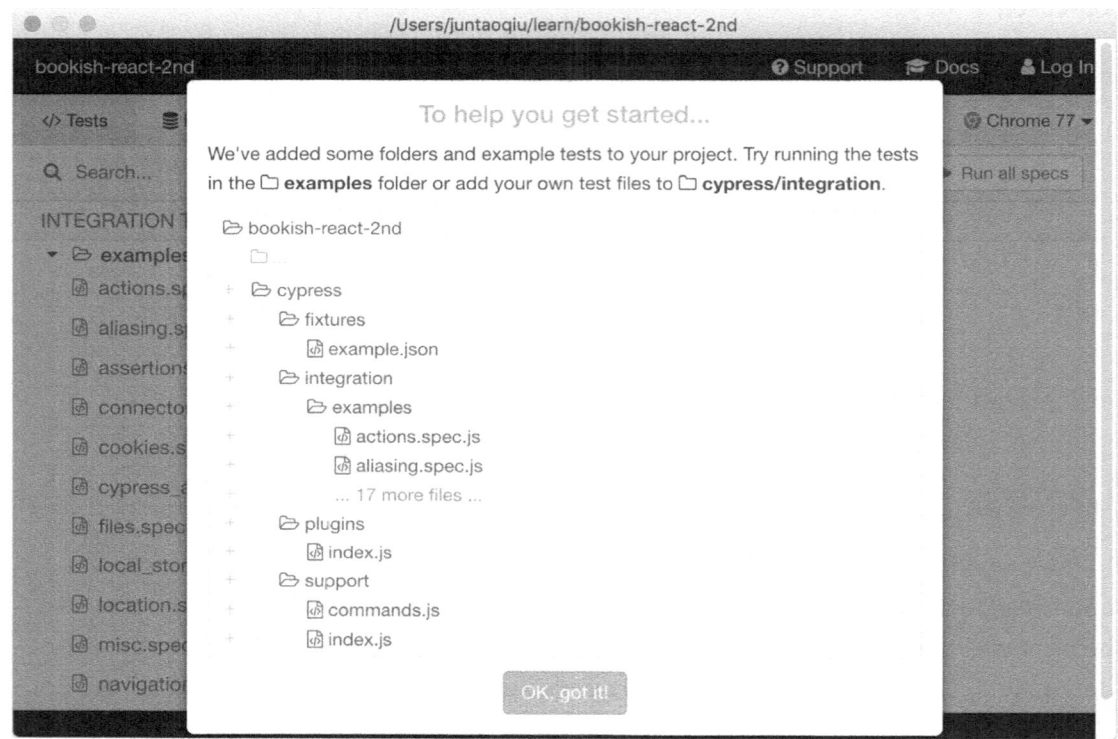

Figure 4-4. *The introduction page of cypress*

This will create a new folder called `cypress` outside of our project code.

For now, let's get rid of most of the generated code and create a file `bookish.spec.js` under the `ui` folder, which is under `cypress/integration` for our first end-to-end test. The folder structure should look like Figure 4-5.

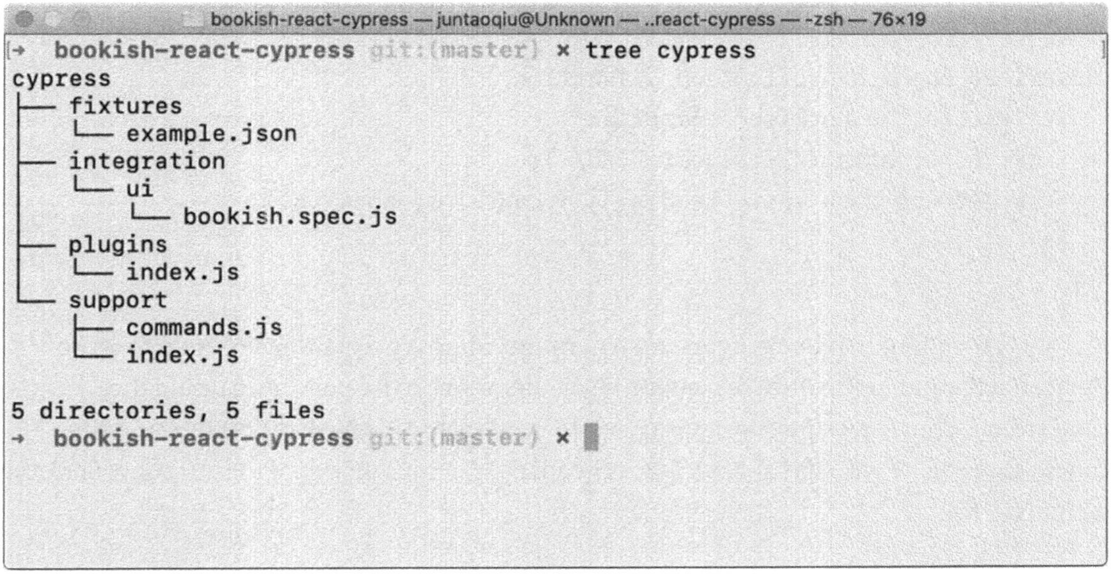
bookish-react-cypress — juntaoqiu@Unknown — ..react-cypress — -zsh — 76×19
→ bookish-react-cypress git:(master) ✗ tree cypress
cypress
├── fixtures
│   └── example.json
├── integration
│   └── ui
│   └── bookish.spec.js
├── plugins
│   └── index.js
└── support
    ├── commands.js
    └── index.js

5 directories, 5 files
→ bookish-react-cypress git:(master) ✗

Figure 4-5. *Folder structure of cypress*

For now, the only thing we need to care about is `bookish.spec.js`. We will examine `fixtures` in the coming chapters.

Writing Our First End-to-End Test

Do you remember when we talked about how the most challenging part of TDD might be where to start and how to write the very first test?

A feasible option for our first test could be

- Make sure there is a `Heading` element on the page, and the content is `Bookish`.

This test might look pointless at first glance, but actually, it can make sure that

- Front-end code can compile and translate.
- The browser can render our page correctly (without any script errors).

So, in our bookish.spec.js, simply put

```
describe('Bookish application', function() {
  it('Visits the bookish', function() {
    cy.visit('http://localhost:3000/');
    cy.get('h2[data-test="heading"]').contains('Bookish')
  })
})
```

cy is the global object in cypress. It contains almost everything we need to write tests: navigating to the browser, querying an element on the page, and doing the assertions. The test we just wrote is trying to visit http://localhost:3000/ and then make sure the h2 with data-test flag as heading has content equal to the string: Bookish (Figure 4-6).

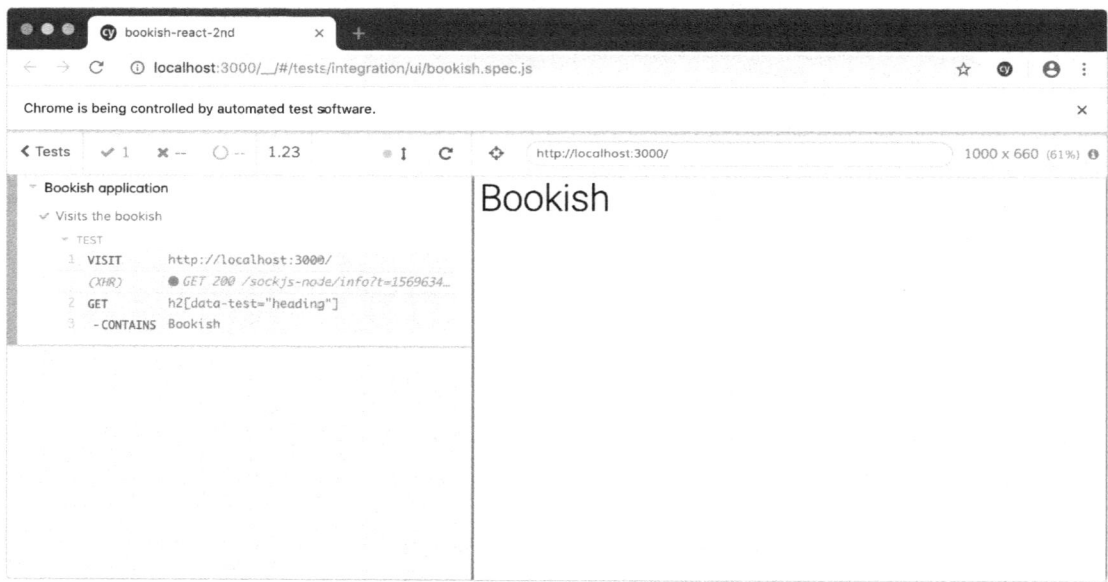

Figure 4-6. *Run our first test*

In the daily development workflow, especially when there are several end-to-end tests running, you might not want to see all the details (fill out form fields, scroll the pages or some notifications), so you can configure it to run in headless mode with the following command:

```
npx cypress run
```

Define a Shortcut Command

Just define a new task under the `scripts` section in `package.json`:

```
"scripts": {
  "e2e": "cypress run"
},
```

Make sure the app is running (`npm start`), and then run `npm run e2e` from another terminal. This will do all the dirty work for you and give you a detailed report after all tests are complete (Figure 4-7).

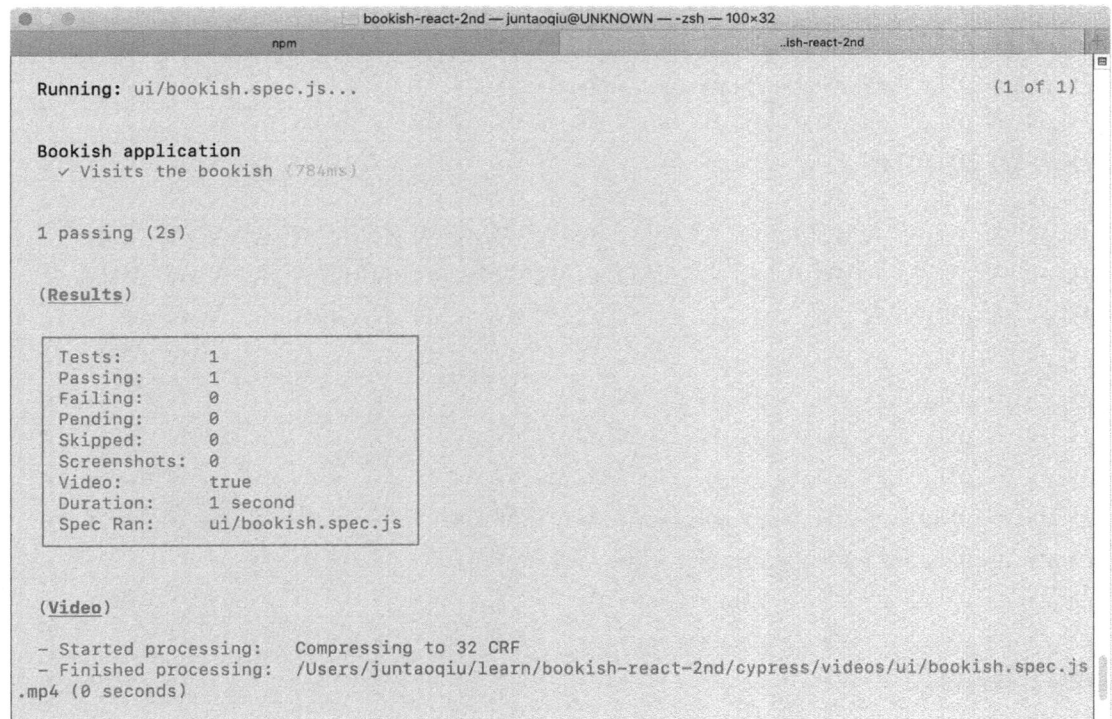

Figure 4-7. *Running end-to-end test in terminal*

As a bonus, you can use this `command` in the CI environment as well.

Commit Code to Version Control

Beautiful! We now have an acceptance test and its corresponding implementation, and we can commit the code to version control just in case we need to look back in the future. I'm going to use `git` in this book since it's the most popular one, and you will find it installed in almost every developer's computer nowadays.

Running the following command will initialize the current folder as a `git` repository:

```
git init
```

Then commit it locally. Of course, you may want to also push it to some remote repository like GitHub or GitLab to share it with colleagues:

```
git add .
git commit -m "make the first e2e test pass"
```

Files to Ignore

If you have something you don't want to be published or shared with others, create a `.gitignore` text file in the root directory, and put the filename you don't want to be shared in it, like so:

```
*.log
.idea/
debug/
```

The list mentioned earlier will ignore any files with `log` extension and folder `.idea` (it's autogenerated by JetBrains IDEs like WebStorm).

Summary

Now look at what we've got:

- A running acceptance test suite

- A page that can render `Bookish` as the `heading`

It's a great achievement. Now, we have all the necessary mechanisms set up, and we can focus on the implementation of the business requirements.

CHAPTER 5

Implementing the Book List

Our first requirement is to develop a book list. From the perspective of the acceptance tests, all we have to do is to make sure that the page contains a list of books – we don't need to worry about what technology will be used to implement the page. And it doesn't matter if the page is dynamically generated or just static HTML, as long as there is a list of books on the page.

Acceptance Tests for Book List

A List (of Books)

First things first, let's add a test case in `bookish.spec.js` within the `describe` block:

```
it('Shows a book list', () => {
  cy.visit('http://localhost:3000/');
  cy.get('div[data-test="book-list"]').should('exist');
  cy.get('div.book-item').should('have.length', 2);
})
```

We expect that there is a container that has the `data-test` attribute of `book list` and that this container has several `.book-item` elements. If we run the test now (`npm run e2e`), it will fail miserably. Following the steps of TDD, we need to implement the simplest possible code to make the test pass:

```
<Typography variant='h2' component='h2' data-test='heading'>
Bookish
</Typography>
```

© Juntao Qiu 2021
J. Qiu, *Test-Driven Development with React*, https://doi.org/10.1007/978-1-4842-6972-5_5

```
+       <div data-test='book-list'>
+         <div className='book-item'>
+         </div>
+         <div className='book-item'>
+         </div>
+       </div>
      </div>
    );
 }
```

Verify Book Name

Great, the test is now passing. As you can see, we have *driven* the HTML structure through the test. Now let's add another expectation to the test:

```
    cy.get('div[data-test="book-list"]').should('exist');
-   cy.get('div.book-item').should('have.length', 2);
+   cy.get('div.book-item').should((books) => {
+     expect(books).to.have.length(2);
+
+     const titles = [...books].map(x => x.querySelector('h2').innerHTML);
+     expect(titles).to.deep.equal(['Refactoring', 'Domain-driven
      design'])
+   })
  })
```

To make this test pass, we can again hard-code the html we expect:

```
  <div data-test='book-list'>
    <div className='book-item'>
+     <h2 className='title'>Refactoring</h2>
    </div>
    <div className='book-item'>
+     <h2 className='title'>Domain-driven design</h2>
    </div>
  </div>
```

Awesome! Our tests pass again (Figure 5-1).

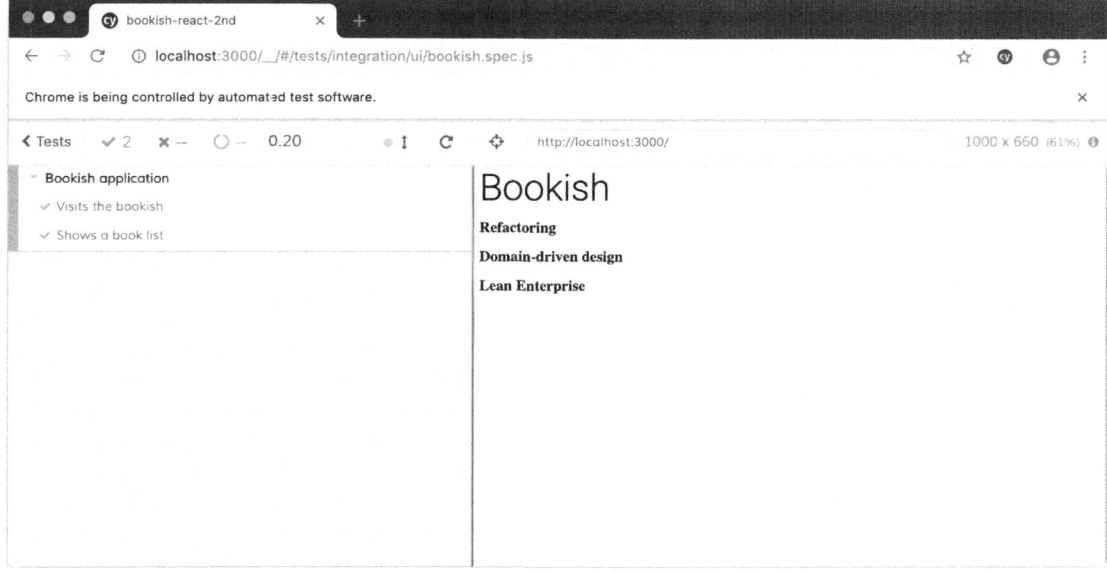

Figure 5-1. *Passing tests with hard-coded book titles*

Now it's time to review the code to check if there are any code smells and then undertake any necessary refactoring.

Refactoring – Extract Function

Firstly, putting all the `.book-item` elements in the `render` method might not be ideal. Instead, we can use a `for` loop to generate the HTML content.

The static repetition is not acceptable to a developer who cares about clean code, right? So we can extract it out as a variable (`books`) and perform a `map` instead:

```
 function App() {
+  const books = [{ name: 'Refactoring' }, { name: 'Domain-driven design'
}];
+
   return (
     <div>
       <Typography variant='h2' component='h2' data-test='heading'>
```

```
      Bookish
      </Typography>
      <div data-test='book-list'>
-       <div className='book-item'>
-         <h2 className='title'>Refactoring</h2>
-       </div>
-       <div className='book-item'>
-         <h2 className='title'>Domain-driven design</h2>
-       </div>
+       {
+         books.map(book => (<div className='book-item'>
+           <h2 className='title'>{book.name}</h2>
+         </div>))
+       }
      </div>
    </div>
  );
```

After that, we can extract the map block into a function that is in charge of render books by any number of given book objects:

```
const renderBooks = (books) => {
  return <div data-test='book-list'>
    {
      books.map(book => (<div className='book-item'>
        <h2 className='title'>{book.name}</h2>
      </div>))
    }
  </div>;
}
```

Note   Review the extract function here, https://refactoring.com/catalog/extractFunction.html

Whenever the method is invoked, we can pass an array of books like so:

```
    <Typography variant='h2' component='h2' data-test='heading'>
    Bookish
    </Typography>
-   <div data-test='book-list'>
-   {
-     books.map(book => (<div className='book-item'>
-       <h2 className='title'>{book.name}</h2>
-     </div>))
-   }
-   </div>
+   {renderBooks(books)}
  </div>
);
```

Our tests are still passing. We improved our internal implementation without modifying the external behavior. This is a good demonstration of just one of the benefits TDD provides: easier and safer cleanup.

Refactoring – Extract Component

Now, the code is much more clean and compact, but it could be better. One possible change is to modularize the code further; the granularity of abstraction should be based on component, rather than on function. For instance, we are using the function renderBooks to render a parsed array as a book list, and we can abstract a component named BookList to do the same thing. Create a file BookList.js, and move the function renderBooks into it.

From React 16 onward, in most cases, we don't need a class when creating a component. By using a pure function, it can be done much more easily (and with less code).

```
import React from 'react';

const BookList = ({books}) => {
  return <div data-test='book-list'>
    {
      books.map(book => (<div className='book-item'>
        <h2 className='title'>{book.name}</h2>
      </div>))
    }
  </div>;
}

export default BookList;
```

Now, we can use this customized component just as we would any React built-in component (e.g., div or h1):

```
function App() {
  const books = [
    { name: 'Refactoring' },
    { name: 'Domain-driven design' }
  ];

  return (
    <div>
      <Typography variant='h2' component='h2' data-test='heading'>
      Bookish
      </Typography>
      <BookList books={books} />
    </div>
  );
}
```

With this refactoring, our code becomes more declarative and also easier to understand. Additionally, our tests remain green. You can fearlessly change the code without worrying about breaking existing functionalities. It gives you confidence to change existing code and improve the internal quality.

Talk to the Book Server

Generally speaking, the data of the book list should never be hard-coded in the code. In most real-life projects, this data is stored somewhere remotely on a server and needs to be fetched when the application launches. To make our application work in that way, we need to do the following:

- Configure a stub server to provide the book data we need.

- Use client-side network library axios to fetch data from the stub server.

- Use the data fetched to render our component.

Although we can simply use native API fetch to communicate with the server side, I prefer axios in this case because it provides semantic API (axios.get, axios.put, and so on), and it has abstractions and shims to block the differences between different browsers (and same browser in different versions).

So let's look into the stub server first.

Stub Server

A stub server is commonly used in the development process. Here, we'll use a tool called json-server. It's a very lightweight and easy-to-get-started node package.

Set Up json-server

Firstly, we need to install it into global space just as we did other tools:

```
npm install json-server --global
```

Then, we will create an empty folder named stub-server:

```
mkdir -p stub-server
cd stub-server
```

After that, we create a db.json file with the following content:

```
{
  "books": [
    { "name": "Refactoring" },
    { "name": "Domain-driven design" }
  ]
}
```

This file defines a route and data for that route. Now, we can launch the server with the following command:

```
json-server --watch db.json --port 8080
```

If you open your browser and navigate to http://localhost:8080/books, you should be able to see something like this:

```
[
  {
    "name": "Refactoring"
  },
  {
    "name": "Domain-driven design"
  }
]
```

Of course, you can use curl to fetch it from the command line.

Make Sure Stub Server Is Working

To verify if the stub server works as expected, we can test it by running curl like so, and we should be able to see the response we set up in the earlier section:

```
$ curl http://localhost:8080/books

[
  {
    "name": "Refactoring"
  },
```

```
{
    "name": "Domain-driven design"
  }
]
```

Let's add a script to make life a little easier. Under `scripts` in our `package.json`, add in `scripts` section:

```
"scripts": {
  "stub-server": "json-server --watch db.json --port 8080"
},
```

We can run `npm run stub-server` from our root directory to get our stub server up and running. Sweet! Let's try to make some changes to the bookish application to fetch this data via HTTP calls.

Async Request in Application

Back to the application folder: `bookish-react`. In order to send a request and get data, we need an HTTP client. In this case, we will use `axios`.

Installing `axios` in our project is easy:

```
npm install axios --save
```

Then, we can use it to fetch data in our `App.js` like this:

```
-import React from 'react';
+import React, { useState, useEffect } from 'react;
import Typography from '@material-ui/core/Typography';
+import axios from 'axios';

import BookList from './BookList';

-function App() {
-   const books = [{ name: 'Refactoring' }, { name: 'Domain-driven design' }];
+const App = () => {
+   const [books, setBooks] = useState([]);
+
+   useEffect(() => {
+     const fetchBooks = async () => {
```

```
+        const res = await axios.get('http://localhost:8080/books');
+        setBooks(res.data);
+      };
+
+      fetchBooks();
+  }, []);

     return (
       <div>
```

You probably noticed that while we were at it, we refactored the App component to be a functional component, rather than a class component. This allows us to use the react-hooks APIs: useState and useEffect. The useState is analogous to the this.setState API, while useEffect is used for side effects such as setTimeout or async remote calls. In the callback, we define an effect that sends an async call to localhost:8080/books, and once the data is fetched, setBooks will be called with that data, and finally BookList will be called with books from the state.

You can see some output in the console from the stub server when the books API is reached when we run our application now (Figure 5-2).

```
stub-server — npm run stub-server — npm — node • npm TMPDIR=/var/folders/hz/zb_z8j4556lc_n2rr9dl9nd40000gn/T/...
> stub-server@1.0.0 stub-server /Users/juntaoqiu/writing/stub-server
> json-server --watch db.json --port 8080


 \{^_^}/ hi!

 Loading db.json
 Done

 Resources
 http://localhost:8080/books

 Home
 http://localhost:8080

 Type s + enter at any time to create a snapshot of the database
 Watching...

GET /books 200 7.736 ms - 81
GET /books 200 3.017 ms - 81
GET /books 304 3.386 ms - -
GET /__rules 404 1.733 ms - 2
GET /db 304 0.266 ms - -
```

Figure 5-2. *Launch the stub server*

Setup and Teardown

Let's take a closer look at our code and tests. As you can see, an implicit assumption here is that the tests *know* that the implementation will return two books. The problem with this assumption is that it makes the tests a little mysterious: Why we are expecting expect(books.length).toEqual(2), why not 3? And why are those two books *Refactoring* and *Domain-Driven Design*? That kind of assumption should be avoided or should be clearly explained somewhere in the tests.

One way to do this is to create some fixture data that will be set before each test and cleaned up after each test finishes.

The json-server provides a programmatic way to do it. We can define the behaviors of the stub server with some code.

Extend Stub Book Service with Middleware

We will need to install json-server locally for this step, so run npm install json-server --save-dev from your command line.

In the stub-server folder, create a file named server.js, and add some middleware to it:

```
const jsonServer = require('json-server')
const server = jsonServer.create()
const router = jsonServer.router('db.json')
const middlewares = jsonServer.defaults()

server.use((req, res, next) => {
  if (req.method === 'DELETE' && req.query['_cleanup']) {
    const db = router.db
    db.set('books', []).write()
    res.sendStatus(204)
  } else {
    next()
  }
})
```

```
server.use(middlewares)
server.use(router)

server.listen(8080, () => {
    console.log('JSON Server is running')
})
```

This function will perform some actions based on the request method and query strings received. If the request is a DELETE request and there is a _cleanup parameter in the query string, we will clean the entity by setting the req.entity to an empty array. So when you send a DELETE to http://localhost:8080/books?_cleanup=true, this function will set the books array to empty.

With this code in place, you can launch the server with the following command:

```
node server.js
```

The complete version of the stub server code is hosted here: https://github.com/abruzzi/react-tdd-mock-server

Once we have this middleware in place, we can use it in our test setup and teardown hooks. At the top of bookish.spec.js, inside the describe block, add

```
before(() => {
  return axios
    .delete('http://localhost:8080/books?_cleanup=true')
    .catch((err) => err);
});

afterEach(() => {
  return axios
    .delete('http://localhost:8080/books?_cleanup=true')
    .catch(err => err)
})

beforeEach(() => {
  const books = [
    { 'name': 'Refactoring', 'id': 1 },
    { 'name': 'Domain-driven design', 'id': 2 }
  ]
```

```
  return books.map(item =>
    axios.post('http://localhost:8080/books', item,
      { headers: { 'Content-Type': 'application/json' } }
    )
  )
})
```

Make sure to also import `axios` at the top of the file.

Before all of the tests run, we'll delete anything from the database by sending a DELETE request to this endpoint `'http://localhost:8080/books?_cleanup=true'`. Then before each test is ran, we insert two books into the stub server with a POST request to URL: `http://localhost:8080/books`. Finally, after each test, we will clean them up.

With the stub server running, run the tests and observe what happens in the console.

beforeEach and afterEach Hook

Now, we can modify the data in the setup however we want. For example, we could add another book called *Building Microservices*:

```
beforeEach(() => {
  const books = [
    { 'name': 'Refactoring', 'id': 1 },
    { 'name': 'Domain-driven design', 'id': 2 },
    { 'name': 'Building Microservices', 'id': 3 }
  ]

  return books.map(item =>
    axios.post('http://localhost:8080/books', item,
      { headers: { 'Content-Type': 'application/json' } }
    )
  )
})
```

And expect three books in the test:

```
it('Shows a book list', () => {
  cy.visit('http://localhost:3000/');
  cy.get('div[data-test="book-list"]').should('exist');
```

```
  cy.get('div.book-item').should((books) => {
    expect(books).to.have.length(3);

    const titles = [...books].map(x => x.querySelector('h2').innerHTML);
    expect(titles).to.deep.equal(
      ['Refactoring', 'Domain-driven design', 'Building Microservices']
    )
  })
});
```

Adding a Loading Indicator

Our application is fetching data remotely, and there is no guarantee that the data will return immediately. We would like there to be some indicator of loading time to improve the user experience. Additionally, when there is no network connection at all (or a timeout), we need to show some error messages.

Before we add this to code, let's imagine how we can simulate those two scenarios:

- Slow request

- Request that failed

Unfortunately, neither of those two scenarios are easy to simulate, and even if we can, we have to couple our test with the code very tightly. Let's rethink what we want to do carefully: there are three statuses of the component (loading, error, success), so if we can test the behaviors of those three statuses in an isolated manner, then we can make sure our component is functional.

Refactor First

To make the test easy to write, we need to refactor a little first. Take a look at App.js:

```
import BookList from './BookList';

const App = () => {
  const [books, setBooks] = useState([]);
```

```
  useEffect(() => {
    const fetchBooks = async () => {
      const res = await axios.get('http://localhost:8080/books');
      setBooks(res.data);
    };

    fetchBooks();
  }, []);

  return (
    <div>
      <Typography variant='h2' component='h2' data-test='heading'>
      Bookish
      </Typography>
      <BookList books={books} />
    </div>
  );
}
```

The purpose seems clear for now, but if we want to add more states, the responsibility might be mixed.

Adding More States

If we want to handle cases when we have a loading or error status, we need to introduce more state to the component:

```
 const App = () => {
   const [books, setBooks] = useState([]);
+  const [loading, setLoading] = useState(false);
+  const [error, setError] = useState(false);

   useEffect(() => {
     const fetchBooks = async () => {
-      const res = await axios.get('http://localhost:8080/books');
-      setBooks(res.data);
+      setError(false);
+      setLoading(true);
+
```

```
+      try {
+        const res = await axios.get('http://localhost:8080/books');
+        setBooks(res.data);
+      } catch (e) {
+        setError(true);
+      } finally {
+        setLoading(false);
+      }
     };

     fetchBooks();
   }, []);
```

As we don't necessarily need to show the loading and error for the whole page, we can instead move it into its own component, BookListContainer.js.

Refactor: Extract Component

```
import React, {useEffect, useState} from 'react';
import axios from 'axios';
import BookList from './BookList';
const BookListContainer = () => {
  const [books, setBooks] = useState([]);
  const [loading, setLoading] = useState(false);
  const [error, setError] = useState(false);

  useEffect(() => {
    const fetchBooks = async () => {
      setError(false);
      setLoading(true);

      try {
        const res = await axios.get('http://localhost:8080/books');
        setBooks(res.data);
      } catch (e) {
        setError(true);
      } finally {
```

```
        setLoading(false);
      }
    };

    fetchBooks();
  }, []);

  return <BookList books={books} />
}

export default BookListContainer;
```

Then the app becomes

```
const App = () => {
  return (
    <div>
      <Typography variant='h2' component='h2' data-test='heading'>
        Bookish
      </Typography>
      <BookListContainer/>
    </div>
  );
}
```

Hmm, it's feasible. But the disadvantage is that we are still coupling the network request with the rendering. This makes the unit test very complex. So let's separate the network and render.

Define a React Hook

Luckily, React allows us to define our hooks in a very flexible way. We can extract the network part out into a hook inside a hooks.js file and allow the component to use it like any other hook.

```
export const useRemoteService = (initial) => {
  const [data, setData] = useState(initial);
  const [loading, setLoading] = useState(false);
  const [error, setError] = useState(false);
```

```
  useEffect(() => {
    const fetchBooks = async () => {
      setError(false);
      setLoading(true);

      try {
        const res = await axios.get('http://localhost:8080/books');
        setData(res.data);
      } catch (e) {
        setError(true);
      } finally {
        setLoading(false);
      }
    };

    fetchBooks();
  }, []);

  return {data, loading, error};
}
```

Here, we split all the network-related code out into a hook. In the BookListContainer, we can invoke it like this:

```
const BookListContainer = () => {
  const {data, loading, error} = useRemoteService([]);

  // if(loading) {
  //   return <p>Loading...</p>
  // }

  // if(error) {
  //   return <p>Error...</p>
  // }

  return <BookList books={data} />
}
```

Looks pretty cool, right? The only parameter required by useRemoteService is the default value for BookList to render. The code is nice and clean now, and most importantly, the functional tests are still passing.

Use the useRemoteService Hook

Additionally, I prefer to put all the UI elements together, which can make the unit tests more convenient:

```
const BookListContainer = () => {
  const {data, loading, error} = useRemoteService([]);
  return <BookList books={data} loading={loading} error={error}/>
}
```

We pass loading and error statuses to the BookList component and let it decide what to display. Before we jump directly into the implementation, let's write some unit tests for those scenarios.

Unit Test with React-Testing-Library

Before we add any unit tests, we need to add some packages:

```
npm install @testing-library/react --save-dev
```

Test Loading State

Now, create a test file inside src called BookList.test.js:

```
import React from 'react'
import {render} from '@testing-library/react'

import BookList from './BookList';

describe('BookList', () => {
  it('loading', () => {
    const props = {
      loading: true
    };
```

```
    const {container} = render(<BookList {...props} />)
    const content = container.querySelector('p');
    expect(content.innerHTML).toContain('Loading');
  });
});
```

Run the test with npm test. Since we don't have the code yet, the test will fail.

We can implement a quick solution:

```
const BookList = ({loading, books}) => {
  if(loading) {
    return <p>Loading...</p>
  }

  return <div data-test='book-list'>
    {
      books.map(book => (<div className='book-item'>
        <h2 className='title'>{book.name}</h2>
      </div>))
    }
  </div>;
}
```

Test Error State

To test the network error case, and you can see now all the tests are passing in Figure 5-3

```
it('error', () => {
  const props = {
    error: true
  };
  const {container} = render(<BookList {...props} />);
  const content = container.querySelector('p');
expect(content.innerHTML).toContain('Error');
})
```

```
bookish-react-2nd — npm run test — node ‹ npm TMPDIR=/var/folders/hz/zb_z8j4556lc_n2rr9dl9nd40000gn/T/ XP...
         npm                              npm                      ..h-react-v2-en

PASS  src/BookList.test.jsx
  BookList
    ✓ loading (19ms)
    ✓ error (1ms)

Test Suites: 1 passed, 1 total
Tests:       2 passed, 2 total
Snapshots:   0 total
Time:        1.095s, estimated 2s
Ran all test suites.

Watch Usage: Press w to show more.
```

Figure 5-3. *Tests about error state now passing*

Test Expected Data

Finally, we can add a happy path to make sure our component renders in the success scenario:

```
it('render books', () => {
  const props = {
    books: [
      { 'name': 'Refactoring', 'id': 1 },
      { 'name': 'Domain-driven design', 'id': 2 },
    ]
  };
  const { container } = render(<BookList {...props} />);
  const titles = [...container.querySelectorAll('h2')].map(x =>
  x.innerHTML);
  expect(titles).toEqual(['Refactoring', 'Domain-driven design']);
})
```

You may be wondering if this is a duplication – haven't we already tested this case in the Acceptance test? Well, *yes* and *no*. The cases in the unit tests can be used as documentation; it specifies what arguments the component requires, field names, and types. For example, in the props, we explicitly show that BookList requires an object with a books field, which is an array.

When running the tests, we will see a warning in the console:

```
console.error node_modules/react/cjs/react.development.js:172
  Warning: Each child in a list should have a unique 'key' prop.

  Check the render method of "BookList." See https://fb.me/react-warning-
  keys for more information.
      in div (at BookList.jsx:14)
      in BookList (at BookList.test.jsx:32)
```

This is telling us that when rendering a list, React requires a unique key for each of the items, such as id. We can quickly fix it by adding a key for each item in the loop. In our case, as each book has a unique ISBN (the International Standard Book Number), we can use it in the stub server. Now, our **final** version of BookList looks like this:

```
import React from 'react';

const BookList = ({loading, error, books}) => {
  if(loading) {
    return <p>Loading...</p>
  }

  if(error) {
    return <p>Error...</p>
  }

  return <div data-test='book-list'>
    {
      books.map(book => (<div className='book-item' key={book.id}>
        <h2 className='title'>{book.name}</h2>
      </div>))
    }
  </div>;
}

export default BookList;
```

All unit tests are passing (Figure 5-4), great!

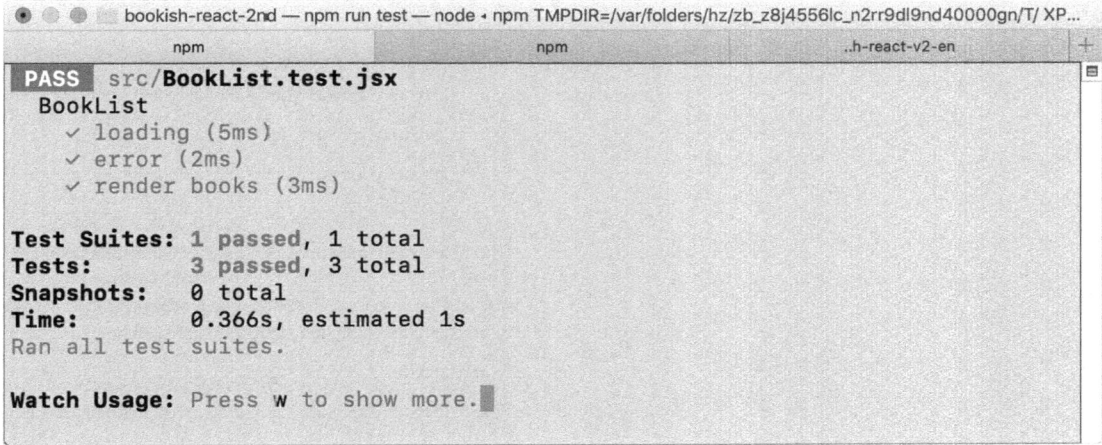

Figure 5-4. *Tests for different states of BookList*

Summary

Sometimes, we may find that it's complicated to write tests for code: there may be a lot of external dependencies. In this case, we need to refactor first, extract the dependencies out, and then add tests.

CHAPTER 6

Implementing the Book Detail View

For each book in the book list, we want to display its name as a hyperlink, so when a user clicks it, the browser will navigate to the detail page. The detail page will contain content specific to each book, including its title, cover image, description, reviews, and so on.

Acceptance Tests

We can describe this requirement as an acceptance test in our `bookish.spec.js`:

```
it('Goes to the detail page', () => {
  cy.visit('http://localhost:3000/');
  cy.get('div.book-item').contains('View Details').eq(0).click();
  cy.url().should('include', '/books/1');
});
```

Run the test, and it will fail.

Link to Detail Page

That is because we don't have a /books route yet, and we don't have the link either. To make the test pass, add a hyperlink in the `BookList` component:

```
      {
        books.map(book => (<div className='book-item' key={book.id}>
          <h2 className='title'>{book.name}</h2>
+         <a href={`/books/${book.id}`}>View Details</a>
        </div>))
      }
```

© Juntao Qiu 2021
J. Qiu, *Test-Driven Development with React*, https://doi.org/10.1007/978-1-4842-6972-5_6

Verify Book Title on Detail Page

Then, to make sure the page shows the expected content after navigation, we need to add a line to bookish.spec.js:

```
  it('Goes to the detail page', () => {
    cy.visit('http://localhost:3000/');
    cy.get('div.book-item').contains('View Details').eq(0).click();
    cy.url().should('include', '/books/1');
+   cy.get('h2.book-title').contains('Refactoring');
  });
```

That checks the page has a .book-title section, and its content is Refactoring. The test fails again; let's fix it by adding client-side routing to our application.

As you can see, there is a page navigation here: the user will be able to jump to the detail page when clicking a button. That means we need some mechanism to maintain the router.

Front-End Routing

We need to add react-router and react-router-dom as dependencies, and they provide the client-side routing mechanism for us:

```
npm install react-router react-router-dom
```

In index.js, we import BrowserRouter and wrap it around <App />. This means the whole application can share the global Router configurations.

```
+import {BrowserRouter as Router} from 'react-router-dom'
+
-ReactDOM.render(<App />, document.getElementById('root'));
+ReactDOM.render(<Router>
+  <App />
+</Router>, document.getElementById('root'));
```

We then define two routes in App.js:

```
+import {Route, Switch} from 'react-router-dom';
 import BookListContainer from './BookListContainer';
+import BookDetailContainer from './BookDetailContainer';

 const App = () => {
   return (
@@ -8,7 +10,10 @@ const App = () => {
       <Typography variant='h2' component='h2' data-test='heading'>
       Bookish
       </Typography>
-      <BookListContainer/>
+      <Switch>
+        <Route exact path='/' component={BookListContainer} />
+        <Route path='/books/:id' component={BookDetailContainer} />
+      </Switch>
     </div>
   );
 }
```

With those routes, when the user accesses root path / , the component BookListContainer will be rendered. When /books/123 is visited, BookDetailContainer will be displayed.

BookDetailContainer Component

Finally, we need to create a new file BookDetailContainer.js. It will be pretty similar to the first version of BookListContainer.js, except that the id of the book will be passed through react-router as match.params.id. Once we have the book id, we can send an HTTP request to load the book details:

```js BookDetailContainer.js

import React, {useEffect, useState} from 'react'
import axios from 'axios'
const BookDetailContainer = ({match}) => { const [id, _] = useState(match.
params.id); const [book, setBook] = useState({});
```

```
useEffect(() => { const fetchBook = async () => { const book = await axios.
get(http://localhost:8080/books/${id}); setBook(book.data); };
fetchBook();
}, [id]);
return (
<h2 className='book-title'>{book.name}</h2>
) }
export default BookDetailContainer ```
```

Great, the functional tests are now passing (Figure 6-1).

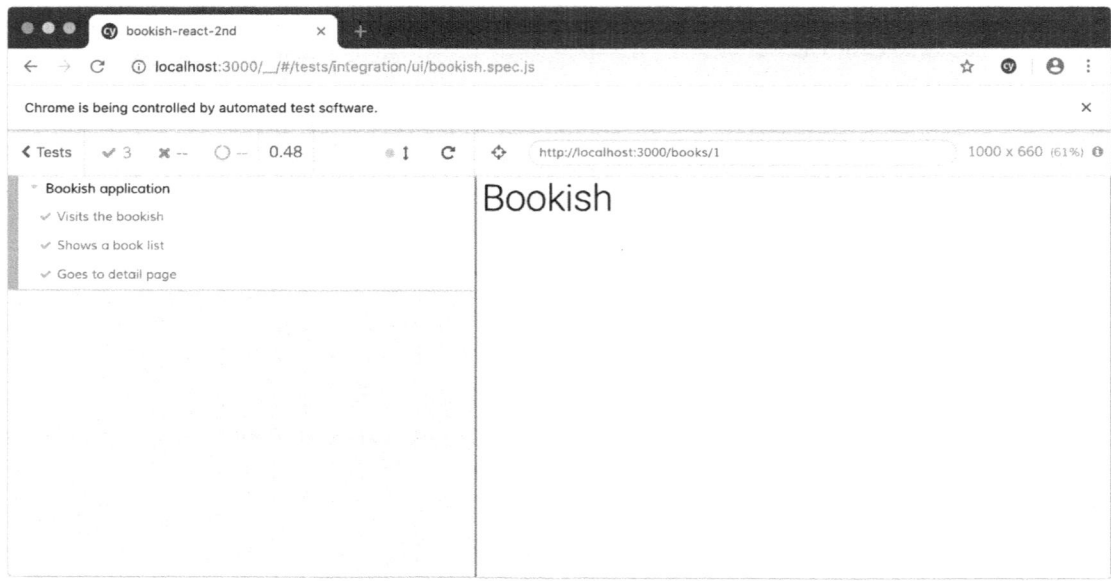

Figure 6-1. *Acceptance test for book detail page*

Generalize useRemoteService Hook

However, the data-fetching process could be improved. It's time for us to refactor the useRemoteService to fit the new requirement. Because we have higher-level tests ready, we can confidently make some changes.

```
-export const useRemoteService = (initial) => {
+export const useRemoteService = (url, initialData) => {
   const [data, setData] = useState(initialData);
```

```
   const [loading, setLoading] = useState(false);
   const [error, setError] = useState(false);

       setLoading(true);

       try {
-          const res = await axios.get('http://localhost:8080/books');
+          const res = await axios.get(url);
           setData(res.data);
       } catch (e) {
           setError(true);
```

We moved hard-coded url out as a parameter, and in the calling place, simply put

```
const {data, loading, error} = useRemoteService('http://localhost:8080/
books', []);
```

Simplify BookDetailContainer with the New Hook

And for BookDetailContainer, it then can be simplified as

```
import React from 'react'
import {useRemoteService} from './hooks';

const BookDetailContainer = ({match}) => {
  const {data} = useRemoteService(`http://localhost:8080/books/${match.
  params.id}`, {});

  return (<div className='detail'>
    <h2 className='book-title'>{data.name}</h2>
  </div>)
};

export default BookDetailContainer
```

The code now looks much cleaner.

Unit Tests

In the end-to-end test, we just make sure there is a title in the detail page. If we add more details to the page, such as description and book cover, we check for them in the lower-level test – the unit test. Unit tests run fast and check more for specific details than end-to-end tests, making it easier for developers to debug if something goes wrong.

Refactor

Extract Presentational Component

Even though in BookDetailContainer there is only a single line to render the details, it's a good idea to extract that line out to a separate component – we'll call it BookDetail:

```
import React from 'react';

const BookDetail = ({book}) => {
  return (<div className='detail'>
    <h2 className='book-title'>{book.name}</h2>
  </div>)
}

export default BookDetail;
```

BookDetailContainer can then be simplified as

```
const BookDetailContainer = ({match}) => {
  const {data} = useRemoteService(`http://localhost:8080/books/${match.
  params.id}`, {});
  return (<BookDetail book={data}/>);
};
```

Let's check all the tests now, functional tests are all passing, but depending on the version of react-router and react-testing-library you are using, your unit tests may be read with the following error message:

● BookList › render books

Invariant failed: You should not use <Link> outside a <Router>

MemoryRouter for Testing

To fix that, we need to modify BookList.test.js a little by providing a <MemoryRouter>:

```
 import BookList from './BookList';

+import {MemoryRouter as Router} from 'react-router-dom';
+
+const renderWithRouter = (component) => {
+  return {...render(<Router>
+      {component}
+    </Router>)}
+};
+
```

We add a wrapper inside the render. This will wrap whatever component you passed in inside a MemoryRouter. **Then** we can invoke the renderWithRouter instead of render in all the tests that need to render a Link:

```
it('render books', () => {
  const props = {
    books: [
      { 'name': 'Refactoring', 'id': 1 },
      { 'name': 'Domain-driven design', 'id': 2 },
    ]
  };
  const { container } = renderWithRouter(<BookList {...props} />);
  const titles = [...container.querySelectorAll('h2')].map(x =>
  x.innerHTML);
  expect(titles).toEqual(['Refactoring', 'Domain-driven design']);
})
```

Book Detail Page

Book Title

Now, we can quickly add unit tests in file BookDetail.test.js, in order to drive the implementation:

```
describe('BookDetail', () => {
  it('renders title', () => {
    const props = {
      book: {
        name: 'Refactoring'
      }
    };

    const {container} = render(<BookDetail {...props} />);

    const title = container.querySelector('.book-title');
    expect(title.innerHTML).toEqual(props.book.name);
  })
});
```

This test will pass because we already render the name field.

Book Description

Let's add some more fields:

```
it('renders description', () => {
  const props = {
    book: {
      name: 'Refactoring',
      description: "Martin Fowler's Refactoring defined core ideas and
      techniques " +
        "that hundreds of thousands of developers have used to improve " +
        "their software."
    }
  };
```

```
const { container } = render(<BookDetail {...props} />);

const description = container.querySelector('p.book-description');
expect(description.innerHTML).toEqual(props.book.description);
})
```

A straightforward implementation could look like this:

```
  const BookDetail = ({book}) => {
    return (<div className='detail'>
      <h2 className='book-title'>{book.name}</h2>
+     <p className='book-description'>{book.description}</p>
    </div>)
  }
```

All tests are now passing in beautiful green! Let's move a step back and see if we can make the codebase a bit better. One thing I've noticed is that the whole project structure is a bit exploding as we created more files.

File Structure

Our file structure is quite flat – there is no hierarchy at all as all the files are just there, in one folder. That is a code smell. It makes it very difficult to find what we're looking for. Let's restructure.

Currently, our files look like this:

```
src
├── App.js
├── BookDetail.jsx
├── BookDetail.test.jsx
├── BookDetailContainer.jsx
├── BookList.jsx
├── BookList.test.jsx
├── BookListContainer.jsx
├── hooks.js
└── index.js
```

There are multiple ways to split an application into modules and organize them. I have found splitting the application by `feature` makes the most sense to me after having tried all of the different combinations across various projects.

Modularize

So for now, let's define two separate folders: `BookDetail` and `BookList` for feature one and feature two, respectively.

```
src
├── App.js
├── BookDetail
│   ├── BookDetail.jsx
│   ├── BookDetail.test.jsx
│   └── BookDetailContainer.jsx
├── BookList
│   ├── BookList.jsx
│   ├── BookList.test.jsx
│   └── BookListContainer.jsx
├── hooks.js
└── index.js
```

This is much organized and easy for readers to locate components that need to be changed.

Testing Data

You may find it a little tricky to clean up all the data for functional tests. And when you want to check how the application looks in the browser manually, there is no data at all.

Let's fix this problem by introducing another `database` file for `json-server`:

```
{
  "books": [
    {"name": "Refactoring", "id": 1, "description": "Martin Fowler's
    Refactoring defined core ideas and techniques that hundreds of
    thousands of developers have used to improve their software."},
```

```
{"name": "Domain-driven design", "id": 2, "description": "Explains how
to incorporate effective domain modeling into the software development
process."},
{"name": "Building Microservices", "id": 3, "description": "Author Sam
Newman provides you with a firm grounding in the concepts while diving
into current solutions for modeling, integrating, testing, deploying,
and monitoring your own autonomous services."},
{"name": "Acceptance Test Driven Development with React", "id": 4,
"description": "This book describes how to apply the Acceptance Test
Driven Development when developing a Web Application named bookish with
React / Redux and other tools in react ecosystem."}
  ]
}
```

and save the content as books.json in the stub-server folder. Now, update the
stub-server script in package.json:

```
json-server --watch books.json --port 8080
```

And run the server (Figure 6-2): npm run stub-server.

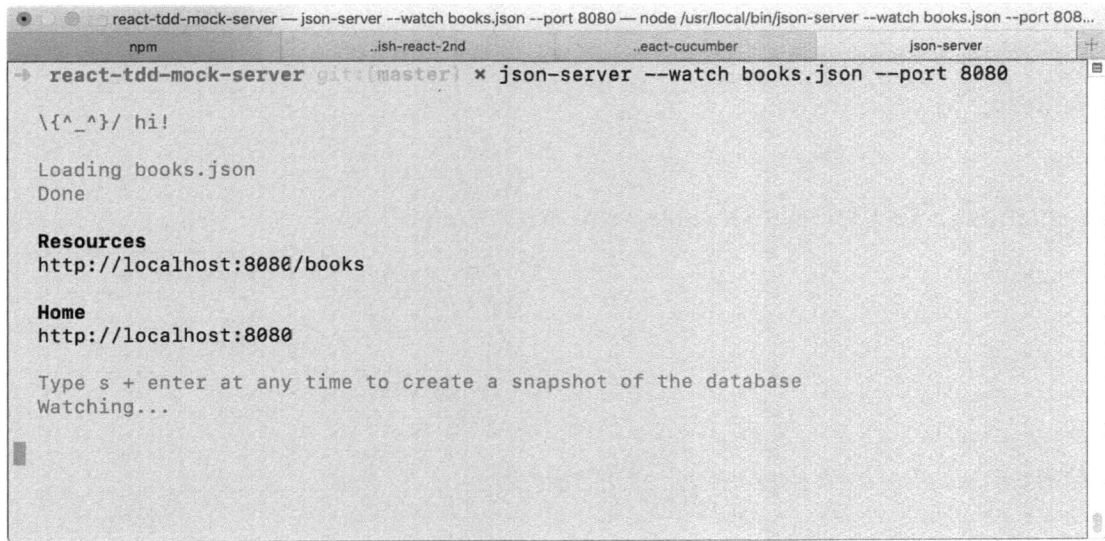

Figure 6-2. *Running our stub server with fake data*

Remember to run the end-to-end tests here as well. As we're changing the data expected in the book list, we'll also need to change what the tests expect. As the server is doing the job of mocking out all the data, you'll notice we don't need the beforeEach and afterEach at this point.

User Interface Refinement

We've now finished two exciting and challenging features. However, the user interface is a little plain (Figure 6-3); let's add some styling.

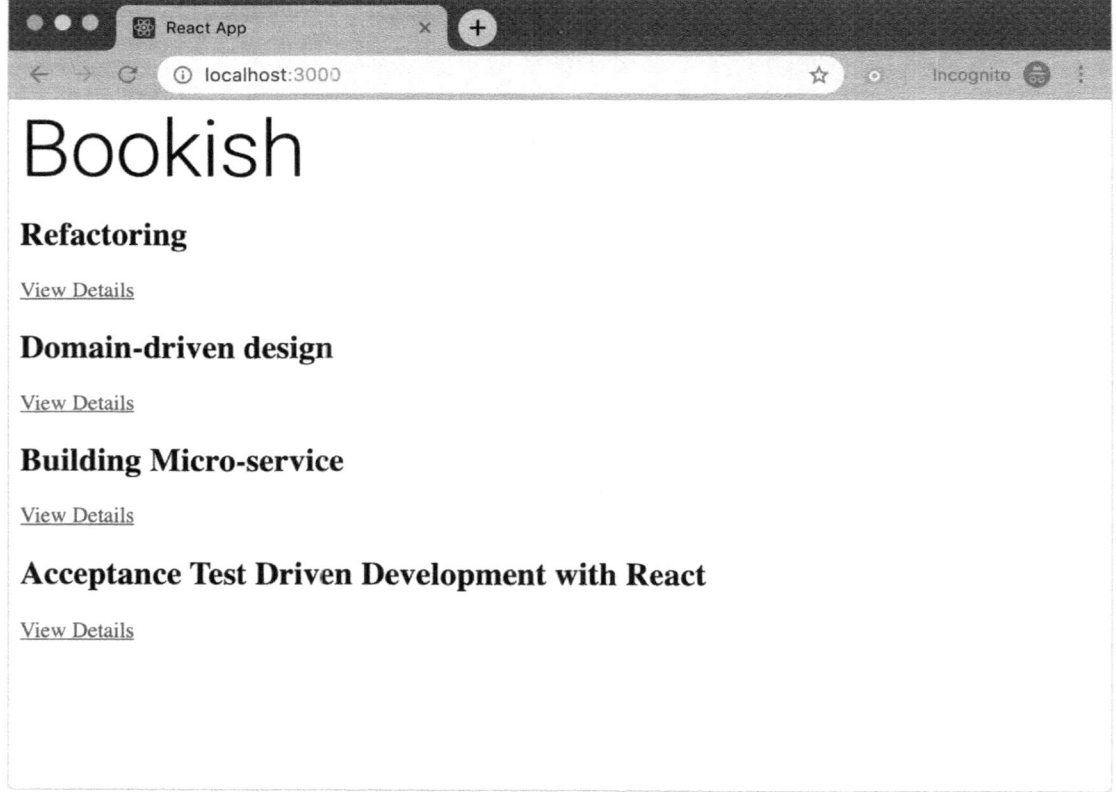

Figure 6-3. *The draft user interface of Bookish*

Material-UI provides many basic and more advanced UI components, along with other helpers such as a `responsive` grid system.

Using `Grid` **System**

In our case, let's implement the `Grid` and `Card` component to our `BookList`:

```
import React from 'react';
+ import {
+   Button,
+   Card,
+   CardActionArea,
+   CardActions,
+   CardContent,
+   Grid,
+   Typography,
+ } from '@material-ui/core';
import { Link } from 'react-router-dom';

const BookList = ({ loading, error, books }) => {
  const classes = useStyles();
  if (loading) {
    return <p>Loading...</p>;
  }

  if (error) {
    return <p>Error...</p>;
  }

-   return <div data-test='book-list'>
-     {
-       books.map(book => (<div className='book-item' key={book.id}>
-         <h2 className='title'>{book.name}</h2>
-         <Link to={`/books/${book.id}`}>View Details</Link>
-       </div>))
-     }
+   return <div data-test='book-list' className={classes.root}>
+     <Grid container spacing={3}>
+       {
+         books.map(book => (<Grid item xs={4} sm={4} key={book.id}
+           className='book-item' >
```

```
+            <Card>
+              <CardActionArea>
+                <CardContent>
+                  <Typography gutterBottom variant='h5' component='h2'
+                  className={classes.name}>
+                    {book.name}
+                  </Typography>
+                  <Typography variant='body2' color='textSecondary'
+                  component='p' className={classes.description}>
+                    {book.description}
+                  </Typography>
+                </CardContent>
+              </CardActionArea>
+              <CardActions>
+                <Button size='small' color='primary'>
+                  <Link to={`/books/${book.id}`}>View Details</Link>
+                </Button>
+              </CardActions>
+            </Card>
+          </Grid>))
+      }
+    </Grid>
   </div>;
 }
```

It may seem a little like a lot, but these are really just markup – think about the HTML tags that fit our application.

Making Styles for Components

In order to do this, we need to use Material-UI's makeStyles function which will link a stylesheet with a function component using the hook pattern (Figure 6-4).

```
const useStyles = makeStyles(theme => ({
  root: {
    flexGrow: 1,
  },
  paper: {
    padding: theme.spacing(2),
    textAlign: 'center',
    color: theme.palette.text.secondary,
  },
  name: {
    maxHeight: 30,
    overflow: 'hidden',
    textOverflow: 'ellipsis',
  },
  description: {
    maxHeight: 40,
    overflow: 'hidden',
    textOverflow: 'ellipsis',
  }
}));
```

At the beginning of the component, we invoke useStyles to generate class names that can be used as className:

```
const classes = useStyles();
```

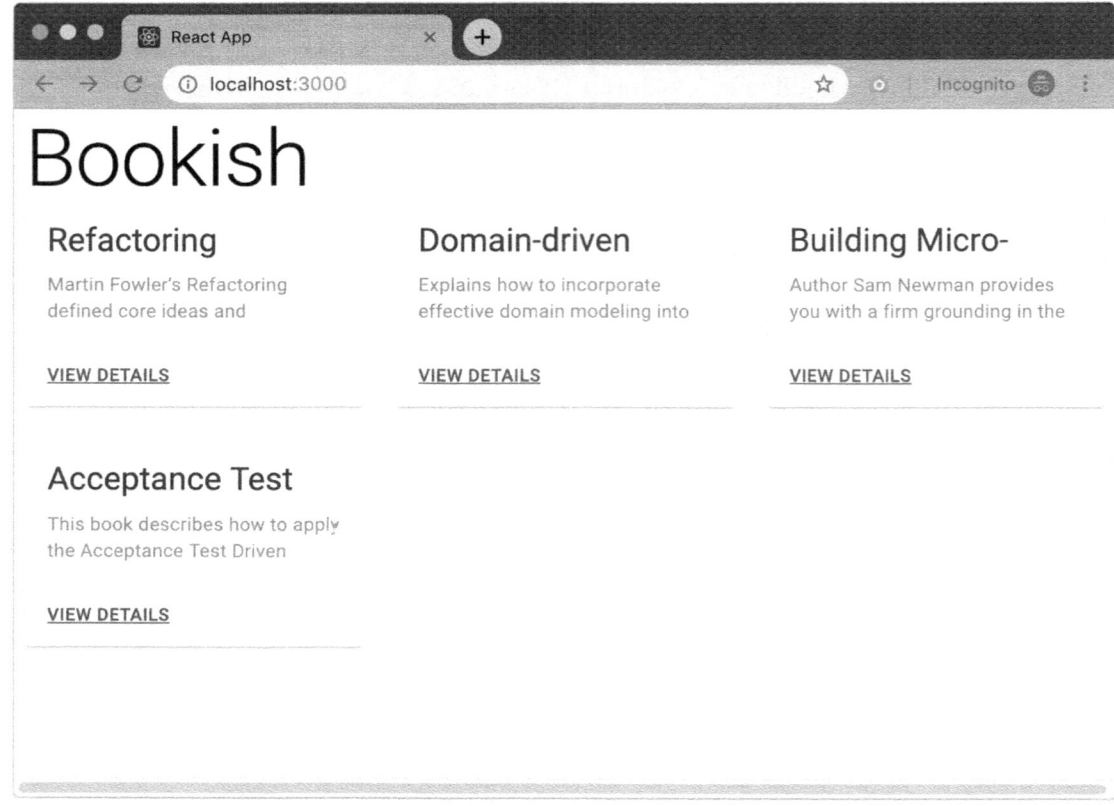

Figure 6-4. *User interface with Material-UI*

Handling default value

Now, we have a requirement adjustment: the data provided by the back-end service may contain some unexpected null values in some of the fields, which we will need to handle gracefully. For example, there is no guarantee that the `description` field is always present (it may be an empty string or null value). In this case, we need to use the book name as the description fallback.

A Failing Test with `undefined`

We can add a test to describe this case, noting the props object doesn't contain `description` field at all:

```
it('displays the book name when no description was given', () => {
```

```
const props = {
  book: {
    name: 'Refactoring'
  }
}
const { container } = render(<BookDetail {...props} />);

const description = container.querySelector('p.book-description');
expect(description.innerHTML).toEqual(props.book.name);
})
```

Then our test failed again (Figure 6-5).

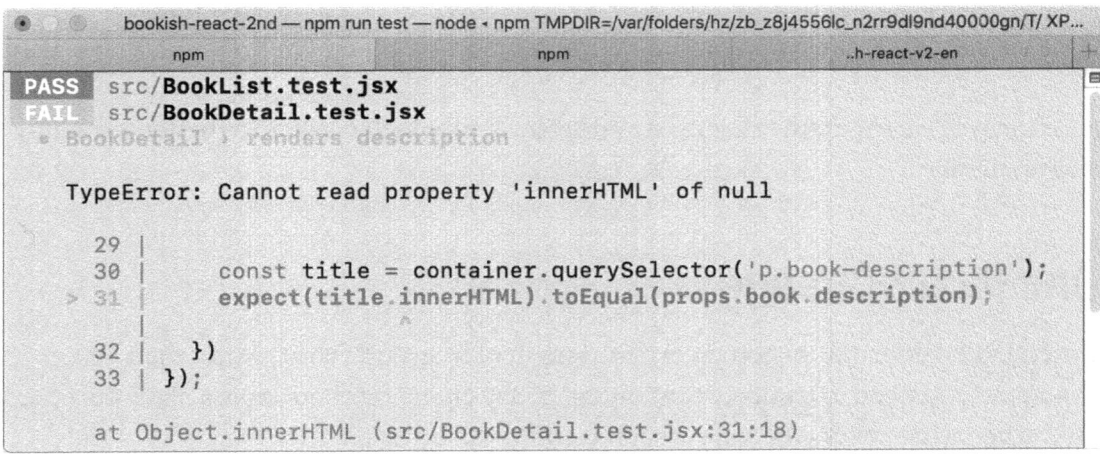

Figure 6-5. *Failed test when data is incomplete*

We can fix that with a conditional operator:

```
const BookDetail = ({book}) => {
  return (<div className='detail'>
    <h2 className='book-title'>{book.name}</h2>
    <p className='book-description'>{book.description ? book.description :
    book.name}</p>
  </div>)
}
```

It's worth noting the `conditional operator` here. It's pretty straightforward for now. But it could go complicated very fast. A better option is to extract that expression out as a separate function. For instance, we can use extract function to isolate that potential change into a pure computing function.

```
const getDescriptionFor = (book) => {
  return book.description ? book.description : book.name;
}

const BookDetail = ({book}) => {
  return (<div className='detail'>
    <h2 className='book-title'>{book.name}</h2>
    <p className='book-description'>{getDescriptionFor(book)}</p>
  </div>)
}
```

That way we separate `rendering` and `computing`, which can lead to better testability and readability.

One Last? Change

Now let's consider another change: if the length of `description` is greater than 300 characters, we need to truncate the content at 300 characters and show a `show more...` link. When a user clicks the link, the full content will be displayed.

We can add a new test for this case:

```
it('Shows *more* link when description is too long', () => {
  const props = {
    book: {
      name: 'Refactoring',
      description: 'The book about how to do refactoring ....'
    }
  };

  const { container } = render(<BookDetail {...props} />);
```

```
const link = container.querySelector('a.show-more');
const title = container.querySelector('p.book-description');

expect(link.innerHTML).toEqual('Show more');
expect(title.innerHTML).toEqual('The book about how to do refactoring
....');
})
```

This drives us to write or modify the code in a way that meets the requirement. Once all the tests pass, we can refactor: extract methods, create new files, move methods or classes around, rename variables or change folder structures, and so on.

It is kind of an *endless* process. There is always room for us to improve. When we have enough time, we can repeat this process until we reach a point where the code is clean and *self-documenting*.

Summary

In this chapter, we've walked through the implementation of Book Detail feature with applying Acceptance Test-Driven Development approach and learned how to iteratively refactor it to an ideal state. Let's dive into more about test with stub techniques in the next chapter.

CHAPTER 7

Searching by Keyword

Our third feature will allow a user to search for a book by its name. This is useful when the book list becomes very long – it can be hard for a user to find what they are looking for when content is more than one screen or page.

Acceptance Test

As previously, we start by writing an `acceptance test`:

```
it('Searches for a title', () => {
  cy.visit('http://localhost:3000/');
  cy.get('div.book-item').should('have.length', 4);
  cy.get('[data-test="search"] input').type('design');
  cy.get('div.book-item').should('have.length', 1);
  cy.get('div.book-item').eq(0).contains('Domain-driven design');
});
```

This test tries to type the keyword `design` into the `search` input box and expects that only `Domain-driven design` will show up in the book list.

The simplest way to implement this feature is to modify the `BookListContainer` by adding a `TextField` from `material-ui` to it:

```
return (<>
  <TextField
    label='Search'
    value={term}
    data-test='search'
    onChange={(e) => setTerm(e.target.value)}
```

© Juntao Qiu 2021
J. Qiu, *Test-Driven Development with React*, https://doi.org/10.1007/978-1-4842-6972-5_7

```
      margin='normal'
      variant='outlined'
    />
    <BookList books={data} loading={loading} error={error}/>
  );
```

We'll need to introduce state to the component – before the return statement, add the following line, remembering to import useState from react:

```
const [term, setTerm] = useState('');
```

When term (the search term) changes, we want to trigger a new search. We can make use of the useEffect hook, something like

```
  useEffect(() => {
    performSearch(`http://localhost:8080/books?q=${term}`)
  }, [term]);
```

We could rewrite each of the axios.get and error and loading steps again here, but it's wiser to reuse the existing useRemoteService we've already defined. Let's tweak it a little first:

```
-export const useRemoteService = (url, initialData) => {
+export const useRemoteService = (initialUrl, initialData) => {
   const [data, setData] = useState(initialData);
+  const [url, setUrl] = useState(initialUrl);
   const [loading, setLoading] = useState(false);
   const [error, setError] = useState(false);

@@ -22,7 +23,7 @@

     fetchBooks();
-  }, []);
+  }, [url]);

-  return {data, loading, error};
+  return {data, loading, error, setUrl};
 }
```

By exporting setUrl, we give the outside world a chance to change the url. Fetching will then be triggered because we define [url] as a dependency for fetchBooks effect.

That means we only need to use `setUrl` in `BookListContainer`, and the hook will do the rest (Figure 7-1):

```
const [term, setTerm] = useState('');
const {data, loading, error, setUrl} = useRemoteService('http://
localhost:8080/books', );

useEffect(() => {
  setUrl(`http://localhost:8080/books?q=${term}`)
}, [term]);
```

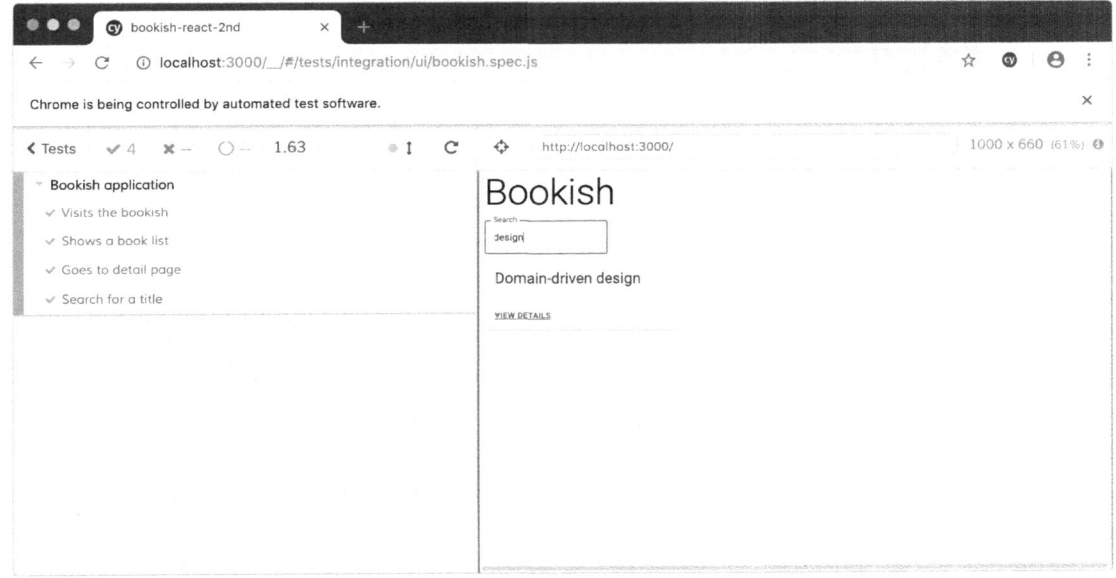

Figure 7-1. *Search for a book*

Note that we are using `books?q=${e.target.value}` as the URL to fetch data. There is a full-text searching API provided by `json-server`; you can send `books?q=domain` to the back end, and it will return all the content that contains the domain.

You can try it on the command line like this:

```
curl http://localhost:8080/books?q=domain
```

Now, our tests are green again. Let's jump to the next step of the `Red-Green-Refactoring`.

One Step Further

Let's say someone else wants to use the search box we just finished on this page; how can we reuse it? It's tough because currently, the search box is very tightly coupled with the rest of the code in BookListContainer, but we can extract it into another component, called SearchBox:

```
import React from 'react';
import TextField from '@material-ui/core/TextField/TextField';

const SearchBox = ({term, onSearch}) => {
  return (<TextField
    label='Search'
    value={term}
    data-test='search'
    onChange={onSearch}
    margin='normal'
    variant='outlined'
  />)
};

export default SearchBox;
```

After that extraction, BookListContainer becomes

```
const onSearch = (event) => setTerm(event.target.value);

return (
  <SearchBox term={term} onSearch={onSearch}/>
  <BookList books={data} loading={loading} error={error}/>
);
```

Now let's add a unit test:

```
import React from 'react';
import {render} from '@testing-library/react';
import userEvent from '@testing-library/user-event';

import SearchBox from './SearchBox';
```

108

```
describe('SearchBox', () => {
  it('renders input', () => {
    const props = {
      term: '',
      onSearch: jest.fn()
    }

    const {container} = render(<SearchBox {...props} />);
    const input = container.querySelector('input[type="text"]');
    userEvent.type(input, 'domain');

    expect(props.onSearch).toHaveBeenCalled();
  });
})
```

Note here that to be able to use user-event, you have to install if you don't have it already:

```
yarn add @testing-library/user-event --dev
```

We are using jest.fn() to create a spy object that can record the trace of invocations. We use userEvent.type API to simulate a change event with domain as it's the payload. We can then expect that onChange method has been called.

Let's add one more requirement here: when performing a search, we don't want white-space be part of the request. So we trim the string before it's sent to service. Let's write a test first:

```
  it('trim empty strings', () => {
    const props = {
      term: '',
      onSearch: jest.fn()
    }

    const {container} = render(<SearchBox {...props} />);
    const input = container.querySelector('input[type="text"]');
    userEvent.type(input, '  ');

    expect(props.onSearch).not.toHaveBeenCalled();
  })
```

It will fail because we currently send any and all `values` to the `books` API. To fix it, we can define a function in `SearchBox` that will `intercept` the event before it reaches the upper level:

```
const protect = (event) => {
  const value = clone(event.target.value);
  if(!isEmpty(value.trim())) {
    return onSearch(event)
  }
}
```

You'll notice that we're using some functions you might not have seen before – `clone` and `isEmpty`. These will need to be installed and imported from lodash.

```
yarn add lodash.isempty lodash.clone
```

And use the function as `onChange` instead of calling `onSearch` directly, and all tests should be passing as showing in Figure 7-2:

```
return (<TextField
  label='Search'
  value={term}
  data-test='search'
  onChange={protect}
  margin='normal'
  variant='outlined'
/>)
```

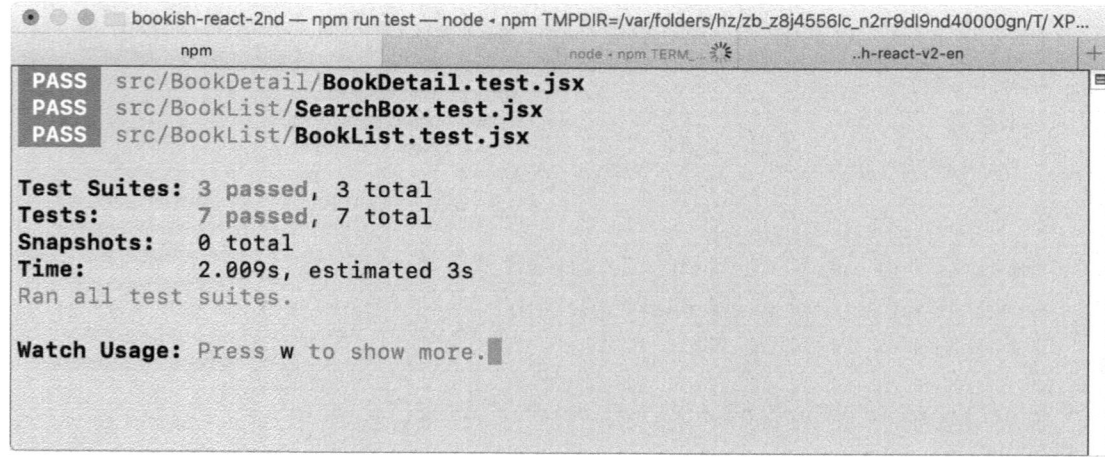

Figure 7-2. *Unit tests for SearchBox*

What Have We Done?

Great, we have finished all the three features! Let's have a quick review of what we've got:

- Three pure components (BookDetail, BookList, SearchBox) and their unit tests

- Two container components (BookDetailContainer, BookListContainer)

- One customized hook for data fetching

- Four acceptance tests to cover the most valuable path (list, detail, and searching)

Moving Forward

Maybe you have already noticed some code smells in our end-to-end tests. We're utilizing many fancy commands without expressing exactly what we are doing in terms of business value:

```
it('Shows a book list', () => {
  cy.visit('http://localhost:3000/');
  cy.get('div[data-test="book-list"]').should('exist');
  cy.get('div.book-item').should((books) => {
    expect(books).to.have.length(3);

    const titles = [...books].map(x => x.querySelector('h2').innerHTML);
    expect(titles).to.deep.equal(['Refactoring', 'Domain-driven design',
'Building Microservices'])
  })
});
```

By introducing a few functions, we can improve the readability significantly:

```
const gotoApp = () => {
  cy.visit('http://localhost:3000/');
}
```

```
const checkAppTitle = () => {
  cy.get('h2[data-test="heading"]').contains('Bookish');
}
```

And in the test cases, we can make use of them like this:

```
it('Visits the bookish', () => {
  gotoApp();
  checkAppTitle();
});
```

For complicated functions, we can abstract even more:

```
const checkBookListWith = (expectation = []) => {
  cy.get('div[data-test="book-list"]').should('exist');
  cy.get('div.book-item').should((books) => {
    expect(books).to.have.length(expectation.length);

    const titles = [...books].map(x => x.querySelector('h2').innerHTML);
    expect(titles).to.deep.equal(expectation)
  })
}
```

And use it like this:

```
const checkBookList = () => {
  checkBookListWith(['Refactoring', 'Domain-driven design', 'Building
  Microservices', 'Acceptance Test Driven Development with React']);
}
```

or

```
const checkSearchedResult = () => {
  checkBookListWith(['Domain-driven design'])
}
```

After we have extracted a few functions, some patterns emerge. We can do some further refactoring:

```
describe('Bookish application', () => {
  beforeEach(() => {
    feedStubBooks();
    gotoApp();
  });

  afterEach(() => {
    cleanUpStubBooks();
  });

  it('Visits the bookish', () => {
    checkAppTitle();
  });

  it('Shows a book list', () => {
    checkBookListWith(['Refactoring', 'Domain-driven design', 'Building
    Microservices']);
  });

  it('Goes to the detail page', () => {
    gotoNthBookInTheList(0);
    checkBookDetail();
  });

  it('Search for a title', () => {
    checkBookListWith(['Refactoring',
      'Domain-driven design',
      'Building Microservices',
      'Acceptance Test Driven Development with React']);
    performSearch('design');
    checkBookListWith(['Domain-driven design']);
  });

});
```

That looks much neater and more concise. Apart from the cleanness, we've also separated the business value and implementation details, which will potentially help us in the future (e.g., if we want to migrate to another testing framework or rewrite some parts of it, the institutions are obvious to the reader).

Summary

In the previous three chapters, we have developed three features of the application `Bookish`, and we have learned how to apply ATDD in a real project. We have learned how to set up the `react` environment quickly and how to use a mock-server to launch the mock service.

We introduced `Cypress` to write `acceptance tests`. Once we have the test, we write simple code to make it pass and refactor when there is code smell found in the code. During the whole process, we keep using the classic `Red-Green-Refactor` cycle. And when we refactor, we split the code based on responsibility and extract methods, rename classes, and restructure the folders to make the code much more compact and easier to read and maintain.

Additionally, we have added some extensions for `json-server` that enable us to prepare some data before running the test cases and clean up after the test finished. That makes the test itself much more readable and independent.

Finally, we learned how to refactor `cypress` commands into meaningful `functions` to improve the readability.

CHAPTER 8

State Management

For a long time, front-end development was all about dealing with the state synchronization of different components. Keywords fulfilled in two search boxes on the page (one at the top and the other at the bottom), the active status of tabs, routing and the hash in the URL, show more... link, and so on. All of that state management can be incredibly confusing. Even when MVVM libraries like Backbone or two-way data binding (one way to share data in your application, use it to listen for events and update values simultaneously between parent and child components) such as in Angular was invented, things were still quite challenging if you had to manage state between different components (if there are components at all – in the world of jQuery, there was no real component, just DOM fragments).

Today, web development is a totally different landscape. In a typical web page, interaction and data translation become even more complicated. And the way to handle those complications has changed too.

© Juntao Qiu 2021
J. Qiu, *Test-Driven Development with React*, https://doi.org/10.1007/978-1-4842-6972-5_8

A Typical UI Scenario

Let's take a look at this simple page in Figure 8-1.

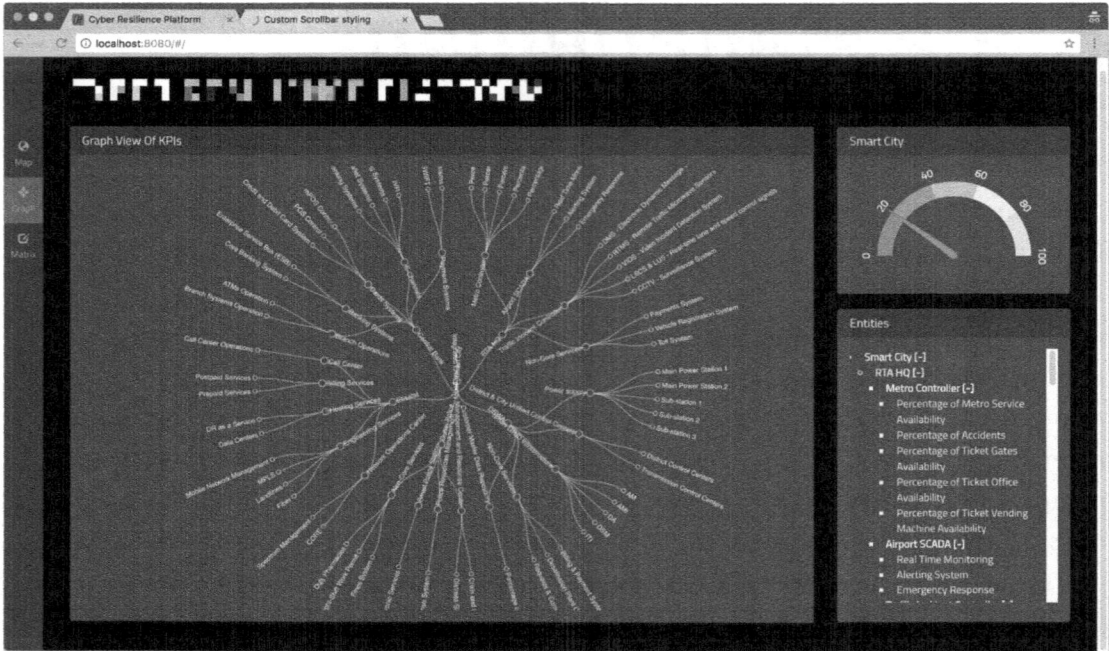

Figure 8-1. *Many components share the same data model behind*

There is a tree component on the right-hand side and a graph component in the middle. Now, when you click a node on the tree, the node should collapse or expand based on its previous status, and the status change should be synched to the graph as well.

If you don't want to use any external library, just using custom events that from the DOM API may cause a dead-loop – when you have to register a listener on graph to listen changes to the tree, also do the same thing to the tree. And when an event is triggered, it will bounce back and forth between those two components. And when you have more than just two components, things will soon go even worse.

A more reliable method is to extract the underlying data and use the pub-sub pattern: the tree and graph are all listening to changes in the data; once the data changes, components should re-render themselves.

Implementations of this pattern are prevalent nowadays; you can find it on almost every web page. You can implement your own pub-sub library; however, you will likely find it tedious and hard to maintain. Fortunately, we have options.

Whenever the underlying data is changed - either by a user event on the browser, a timer, or an async service call - we need an easy way to manage those changes and make sure the data model is always reflected in the latest data across all the components.

A Brief of Redux

Redux is a popular JavaScript state management tool.

As the redux documentation states:

Redux is a predictable state container for JavaScript apps.

By using it, testing and debugging your application becomes straightforward, and you can easily track its state. It's not bound to any library or framework, so while you don't have to use it with React, that is its most common implementation.

Three Principles of Redux

- A single source of truth
- State is read-only
- Changes are made with pure functions

In the Redux world, all state is stored inside a single global data source. At any given time, this data source can be mapped to the view. When changes occur – for example, a user clicks a button, a timeout occurs, or a back-end async message arrives – an action will be created, in the form of an object describing what happened.

Actions are just payloads of information in the form of JavaScript objects that transfer information from our application to our store of state.

Once created, the action will go through a pure function called a reducer. The reducer will specify how the application state will change in response to the action, and that may trigger another re-render of the view. It takes in the previous state and the action and returns the new state. Figure 8-2 demonstrates the process clearly.

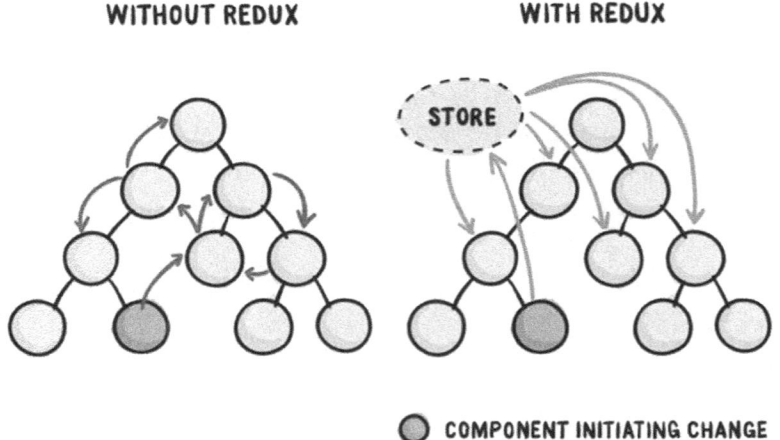

WITHOUT REDUX   **WITH REDUX**

COMPONENT INITIATING CHANGE

Figure 8-2. *Application with or without using redux. Source: Danny Huang (https://kuanhsuh.github.io/2017/09/28/What-s-Redux-and-how-to-use-it/)*

Thanks to the `virtual` dom mechanism provided by React, the UI will re-render with minimal effort.

Decoupling Data and View

If you take a close look at our useRemoteService hook, you will notice that it's actually doing a number of things:

```
export const useRemoteService = (initialUrl, initialData) => {
  const [data, setData] = useState(initialData);
  const [url, setUrl] = useState(initialUrl);
  const [loading, setLoading] = useState(false);
  const [error, setError] = useState(false);

  useEffect(() => {
    const fetchBooks = async () => {
      setError(false);
      setLoading(true);

      try {
        const res = await axios.get(url);
        setData(res.data);
      } catch (e) {
```

```
      setError(true);
    } finally {
      setLoading(false);
    }
  };

  fetchBooks();
}, [url]);

return {data, loading, error, setUrl};
}
```

1. It makes a request for data to an external service.

2. It takes care of url changes.

3. It manages several statuses, including `loading` and `error`.

Some of those statuses will always be updated together, for example:

```
{
  data: [],
  loading: false,
  error: false
}
```

or

```
{
  error: true
}
```

However, it's not immediately obvious at first glance in the code snippet discussed earlier.

Ideally, we could rewrite our container object to trigger some data-fetching action, like in `BookDetailContainer`:

```
const BookDetailContainer = ({match}) => {
  const book = fetchBookById(match.params.id);
  // that will fetch data with `match.params.id`
  return (<BookDetail book={book}/>);
};
```

fetchBookById could be either a synchronous function call or a synchronous remote call, but for BookDetailContainer, it doesn't matter much. As mentioned earlier, along with all the components, in the global space, there is a store (like a database) that maintains application state. Whenever an action is triggered somewhere in the UI, and some modification occurs, then the corresponding updated data is sent to components that need to be re-rendered.

That's how the state management container can help us. The container can handle the details for us, including listening to the changes, dispatching actions, reducing state, and broadcasting changes.

View = f(state)

There is a well-known formula in the React community (interestingly, it seems this pattern has already been discussed well a long time ago in the Desktop GUI context, more to read in "Further Reading" section at the bottom): view = f(state), meaning that view is just a function of state. state here represents a snapshot of our application state. For example, when a user opens the Bookish home page, the data snapshot at that point in time could be

```
const state = {
    books: [
      {'name': 'Refactoring', 'id': 1, 'description': 'Refactoring'},
      {'name': 'Domain-driven design', 'id': 2, 'description': 'Domain-
      driven design'},
      {'name': 'Building Microservices', 'id': 3, 'description': 'Building
      Microservices'}
    ],
    term: ''
}
```

When the user types Domain in the search box, the snapshot becomes

```
const state = {
    books: [
      {'name': 'Domain-driven design', 'id': 2, 'description': 'Domain-
      driven design'}
```

```
  ],
  term: 'Domain'
}
```

These two pieces of data (state) can represent the whole application at a point. Since `view = f(state)`, for any given `state`, the `view` is always predictable, so the only thing the application developer cares about is how to manipulate the data, as the UI will render automatically.

I know that may sound simple, but it only appeared relatively recently in real-world applications (the first release of `redux` was June 2015, barely five years ago).

Implementing State Management

To use redux to handle the state management of our application, we need to address all the three components: action, reducer, and the global store. Let's set up the environment by installing some dependencies first.

Environment Set Up

Firstly, we need to add some packages to enable us to use `redux`:

```
npm install redux redux-thunk history react-router-redux reselect --save
```

Start from `Action`

In `redux`, action is a payload of information that sends data from your application to the store. It's similar to events in other GUI applications. To apply this information to the store, you will have to `dispatch` (send) it.

`action` is an excellent entry point – it will make us consider the way that the components interact with each other and how each component interacts with the outside world.

Take `BookListContainer`, for example. We expect that it has the ability to set the keyword for searching.

Create a folder called redux, and inside a sub-folder called actions, add a file called actions.test.js:

```
import { setSearchTerm } from './actions'

describe('BookListContainer related actions', () => {
  it('Sets the search keyword', () => {
    const term = ''
    const expected = {
      type: 'SET_SEARCH_TERM',
      term
    }
    const action = setSearchTerm(term)
    expect(action).toEqual(expected)
  })
})
```

This test asserts that when a search term is provided to the setSearchTerm action creator, the action will be created.

The action creator, as the name suggests, will create an action and normally will be binded with events from user interaction (mouse click, keyboard).

So at the moment, setSearchTerm is only an empty function in actions.js, but it's very simple to implement here:

```
export const setSearchTerm = (term) => {
  return { type: 'SET_SEARCH_TERM', term }
}
```

Actions have a type property that signal the type of action being performed, but other than that, the structure of the action object is up to us to define.

setSearchTerm takes in a search term, and returns an action of type SET_SEARCH_TERM, and whatever string was provided as the search term.

A piece of cake!

Note that while we are saving term in the store here, we don't have to. It's really up to you – the developer – to decide where to put those statuses. A good rule of thumb is to keep the store as simple and flat as possible. Any data that could be computed by other fields should not be placed there, and in most cases, internal state that no one else cares about should stay inside the component as well.

Async Actions

Things get a little trickier for asynchronous actions. To make these work, we need to configure `redux-thunk` and create a mock `store` (for testing).

Redux-thunk is a middleware (basically, a middleware can intercept all the actions you send to store and manipulate them based on some condition, e.g., do some auditing or logging) that allows action creators to return a function instead of an action. This means that we can delay dispatching the action, or only dispatch based on conditional logic, allowing us to handle asynchronous actions.

Let's add the `redux-mock-store` to our dependencies first:

```
npm install redux-mock-store --save-dev
```

Before we write the tests, we'll create a `mockStore` in `actions.test.js` like this:

```
import configureMockStore from 'redux-mock-store'
import thunk from 'redux-thunk'

const middlewares = [thunk]
const mockStore = configureMockStore(middlewares)
```

Then let's define the happy path that assumes the network is operating, and we can retrieve the data we are fetching (remembering to also import `axios` as we're using it for network requests):

```
it('Fetches data successfully', () => {
  const books = [
    { id: 1, name: 'Refactoring' },
    { id: 2, name: 'Domain-driven design' },
  ];
  axios.get = jest
    .fn()
    .mockImplementation(() => Promise.resolve({ data: books }));

  const expectedActions = [
    { type: 'FETCH_BOOKS_PENDING' },
    { type: 'FETCH_BOOKS_SUCCESS', books },
  ];
```

```
  const store = mockStore({ books: [] });

  return store.dispatch(fetchBooks('')).then(() => {
    expect(store.getActions()).toEqual(expectedActions);
  });
});
```

Here, we expect `fetchBooks` will create two `actions`: one to indicate that the request has been sent and another to indicate a response has been received.

Since the request is using `axios` underneath, we can use `jest.fn().mockImplementation()` to stub it. It will intercept the call to `axios.get` and call whatever function we've defined instead, so we don't send a real HTTP request as part of the test.

```
axios.get = jest.fn().mockImplementation(
  () => Promise.resolve({data: books}))
```

Here is the implementation inside `actions.js`:

```
import axios from 'axios'

export const fetchBooks = () => {
  return (dispatch) => {
    dispatch({type: 'FETCH_BOOKS_PENDING'})
    return axios.get(`http://localhost:8080/books`).then((res) => {
      dispatch({type: 'FETCH_BOOKS_SUCCESS', books: res.data})
    })
  }
}
```

Firstly, we `dispatch` a FETCH_BOOKS_PENDING action and call `axios.get`. When the promise is resolved, we can `dispatch` the FETCH_BOOKS_SUCCESS action with the response as payload.

The Failure Scenario

For the case of a network failure (e.g., a timeout), we can use `jest.fn().mockImplementation()` again in the unit test:

```
axios.get = jest.fn().mockImplementation(
  () => Promise.reject({message: 'Something went wrong'}))
```

Then, verify the failed action is dispatched as expected:

```
it('Fetch data with error', () => {
  axios.get = jest
    .fn()
    .mockImplementation(() =>
      Promise.reject({ message: 'Something went wrong' })
    );

  const expectedActions = [
    { type: 'FETCH_BOOKS_PENDING' },
    { type: 'FETCH_BOOKS_FAILED', err: 'Something went wrong' },
  ];
  const store = mockStore({ books: [] });

  return store.dispatch(fetchBooks('')).then(() => {
    expect(store.getActions()).toEqual(expectedActions);
  });
});
```

We can add a `catch` case in promise `rejected` branch to make our test green:

```
export const fetchBooks = (term) => {
  return (dispatch) => {
    dispatch({type: 'FETCH_BOOKS_PENDING'})
    return axios.get(`http://localhost:8080/books?q=${term}`).then((res) =>
{
      dispatch({type: 'FETCH_BOOKS_SUCCESS', books: res.data})
    }).catch((err) => {
      dispatch({type: 'FETCH_BOOKS_FAILED', err: err.message})
    })
  }
}
```

Searching Action

We are expecting that the action `fetchBooks` can use `term` value from the `store` as the keyword when sending the request, which will enable the filter functionality.

Note that we are setting the term to domain in the mockStore and will need to update the fetchBooks action to account for a query parameter being provided:

```
it('Search data with term', () => {
  const books = [
    { id: 1, name: 'Refactoring' },
    { id: 2, name: 'Domain-driven design' },
  ];
  axios.get = jest
    .fn()
    .mockImplementation(() => Promise.resolve({ data: books }));

  const store = mockStore({ books: [] });

  return store.dispatch(fetchBooks('domain')).then(() => {
    expect(axios.get).toHaveBeenCalledWith(
      'http://localhost:8080/books?q=domain'
    );
  });
});
```

Refactor

There are a lot of hard-coded and "magic" strings in the action test and implementation. We can extract them to some common place so they can be referenced from there. Let's create a file called types.js:

```
export const SET_SEARCH_TERM = 'SET_SEARCH_TERM'
export const FETCH_BOOKS_PENDING = 'FETCH_BOOKS_PENDING'
export const FETCH_BOOKS_SUCCESS = 'FETCH_BOOKS_SUCCESS'
export const FETCH_BOOKS_FAILED = 'FETCH_BOOKS_FAILED'
```

And import it as variable types wherever we want to use it:

```
import * as types from './types'
```

Then, we can use types.FETCH_BOOKS_PENDING to reference it:

```
const expectedActions = [
  { type: types.FETCH_BOOKS_PENDING},
  { type: types.FETCH_BOOKS_SUCCESS, books }
]
```

Reducer

In redux, a reducer is just a pure function – if the input is certain, the output will always be predictable. The reducer is responsible for articulating how the application's state will change in response to any actions sent to the store.

Implementing the reducer is quite simple. For example, FETCH_BOOKS_PENDING and FETCH_BOOK_SUCCESS can be tested like this, inside reducers/reducer.test.js:

```
import reducer from './reducer';
import * as types from '../types';

describe('Reducer', () => {
  it('Show loading when request is sent', () => {
    const initState = { loading: false };

    const action = { type: types.FETCH_BOOKS_PENDING };
    const state = reducer(initState, action);

    expect(state.loading).toBeTruthy();
  });

  it('Add books to state when request successful', () => {
    const books = [
      { id: 1, name: 'Refactoring' },
      { id: 2, name: 'Domain-driven design' },
    ];

    const action = {
      type: types.FETCH_BOOKS_SUCCESS,
      books
    };
```

```
    const state = reducer([], action);
    expect(state.books).toBe(books);
  });
});
```

We're expecting that when FETCH_BOOKS_PENDING action is sent to the reducer, it will set loading to true and that FETCH_BOOKS_SUCCESS will attach the response (the list of books) to state when the request is successful.

```
import * as types from '../types';

const reducer = (state = [], action) => {
  switch (action.type) {
    case types.FETCH_BOOKS_PENDING:
      return { ...state, loading: true };
    case types.FETCH_BOOKS_SUCCESS:
      return { books: action.books };
    default:
      return state;
  }
};
```

```
export default reducer;
```

Testing action creator is just like Value-Object testing in Java, and testing reducer is comparable to testing static util classes. In the React community, people tend to test action+reducer+store together as integration tests instead. Personally, I don't directly test that code at all. They are even explicitly ignored in the modulePathIgnorePatterns section of my package.json.

We'll talk about that more in the next section.

Integration Test for Redux Store

Inside the src folder, create store.test.js:

```
import axios from 'axios';

import * as actions from './redux/actions/actions';
import store from './store';
```

```
describe('Store', () => {
  const books = [
    {id: 1, name: 'Refactoring'}
  ]

  it('Fetch books from remote', () => {
    axios.get = jest.fn().mockImplementation(() => Promise.resolve({data:
    books}))

    return store.dispatch(actions.fetchBooks()).then(() => {
      const state = store.getState()
      expect(state.books.length).toEqual(1)
      expect(state.books).toEqual(books)
    })
  })
})
```

Then, we create `store.js`. We import the `actions` defined earlier, create a real `store` to perform the `dispatch`, and expect it to return the `correct` response. We import the real `reducers` and create a store by using the `createStore` function provided by `redux`:

```
import { applyMiddleware, createStore, compose } from 'redux';
import thunk from 'redux-thunk';

import reducer from './redux/reducers/reducer';

const initialState = {};

const middlewares = [thunk]

const composedEnhancers = compose(
  applyMiddleware(...middlewares)
)

const store = createStore(
  reducer,
  initialState,
  composedEnhancers
)

export default store
```

There's our integration test – it connects `action + reducer + store` together. This kind of test is a little heavier than the other unit tests, but it provides unique value: it demonstrates that each element can work together to provide the expected outcome.

Now that we've connected our actions and reducers to state, let's update our `fetchBooks` action to use state.

```
-export const fetchBooks = (term) => {
+export const fetchBooks = () => {
- return (dispatch) => {
+ return (dispatch, getState) => {
    dispatch({ type: types.FETCH_BOOKS_PENDING });
+   const state = getState();
-   return axios.get(`http://localhost:8080/books?q=${term || ''}`).
then((res) => {
+   return axios.get(`http://localhost:8080/books?q=${state.term || ''}`).
then((res) => {
      dispatch({ type: types.FETCH_BOOKS_SUCCESS, books: res.data });
    }).catch((err) => {
      dispatch({type: types.FETCH_BOOKS_FAILED, err: err.message})
    });
  };
};
```

You will also need to update the mockStore in the `Search data with term` test.

Now, we can add another integration test for our `searching` functionality:

```
it('Performs a search', () => {
  axios.get = jest.fn().mockImplementation(() => Promise.resolve({data:
  books}))
  store.dispatch(actions.setSearchTerm('domain'))

  return store.dispatch(actions.fetchBooks()).then(() => {
    const state = store.getState()

    expect(state.term).toEqual('domain')
    expect(axios.get).toHaveBeenCalledWith('http://localhost:8080/
    books?q=domain')
  })
})
```

Migrating the Application

Our next step is to migrate our application to redux. As we have sufficient acceptance tests, we don't need to worry about breaking any functionality.

Firstly, we need to add react-redux as a dependency:

```
npm install react-redux
```

We pass the store to a Provider component in index.js. This means the whole component tree can share this store at any time:

```
+import { Provider } from 'react-redux';
+import store from './store';

-ReactDOM.render(<Router>
-   <App />
-</Router>, document.getElementById('root'));
+const root = <Provider store={store}>
+   <Router>
+      <App />
+   </Router>
+</Provider>
+
+ReactDOM.render(root, document.getElementById('root'));
```

Since the presentational components are stateless, we leave them as they are – our migration should only affect the container components. For BookListContainer, there will be many changes, as data fetching is delegated to actions:

```
const dispatch = useDispatch();

useEffect(() => {
  dispatch(actions.fetchBooks(term))
}, [term]);
```

useDispatch is shipped with react-redux and can be used to dispatch an action we defined earlier – fetchBooks.

Whenever term state in BookListContainer changes, it will trigger fetchBooks, and once the data is returned from server side, we can use a selector to derive the data we need from state. Because we want to keep our store as lean as possible, in keeping with the principles of good redux architecture, we use a selector. A selector function is a function that accepts the Redux store state as an argument and returns data based on that state.

We can choose to do this with useSelector from redux like

```
const books = useSelector(state => state.books);
```

or define a function to do all the mapping. I prefer the second option, using a library called reselect, as it provides a composable selector and cachable results (which means it will save the computed value internally unless the dependencies of the value have changed), in the form of memorization. That way our application can be more performant, especially for applications that have relatively big store. Let's install it first to the project:

```
npm install reselect
```

Then, we define a selector inside redux/selector:

```
import { createSelector } from 'reselect';

const bookListSelector = createSelector([
  state => state.books,
  state => state.loading,
  state => state.error,
], (books, loading, error) => ({books, loading, error}));

export default bookListSelector;
```

createSelector takes two arguments, an array of input-selectors and a transform function, and returns a memorized selector. Not that our transform function isn't doing much transforming right now, just returning the values directly from state.

Finally, connect them:

```
import bookListSelector from '../../redux/selectors/selector';

const BookListContainer = () => {
  const [term, setTerm] = useState();
  const dispatch = useDispatch();
```

```
  useEffect(() => {
    dispatch(actions.fetchBooks());
  }, [term, dispatch]);

  const onSearch = (event) => {
    dispatch(actions.setSearchTerm(event.target.value));
    dispatch(actions.fetchBooks());
  };

  const { books, loading, error } = useSelector(bookListSelector);

  return (

      <SearchBox term={term} onSearch={onSearch} />
      <BookList books={books} loading={loading} error={error} />

  );
};
```

Test the Container

If you take a close look at BookListContainer, you will find it's relatively difficult to test at the unit-test level. By saying that, I mean it depends on a few outside components like actions and even the network.

We don't want to use the real network, so we need to figure out a way to mock the network. Fortunately, axios-mock-adapter can do this for us.

```
npm install axios-mock-adapter --save-dev
```

Inside BookListContainer.test, import the new dependency and create a new mock. We can define the mock by calling onGet and providing the expected result in reply. In our case, we need two books returned from downstream:

```
  it('renders', async () => {
    const mock = new MockAdapter(axios);
    mock.onGet('http://localhost:8080/books?q=').reply(200, [
      {'name': 'Refactoring', 'id': 1},
      {'name': 'Acceptance tests driven development with React', 'id': 2},
    ]);
```

```
  const {findByText} = renderWithProvider(<BookListContainer/>);

  const book1 = await findByText('Refactoring');
  const book2 = await findByText('Acceptance tests driven development
  with React');

  expect(book1).toBeInTheDocument();
  expect(book2).toBeInTheDocument();
});
```

Note that we use another wrapper function – renderWithProvider – to avoid errors caused by calling useDispatch outside of a provider. Essentially, react-redux expects that hook is being called inside a <Provider>.

```
const renderWithProvider = (component) => {
  return {...render(<Provider store={store}>
     <Router>
       {component}
     </Router>
    </Provider>)}
};
```

Here, we're using the same store as in the real application. Of course, you can define some static store for testing as well.

Additionally, we use the toBeInTheDocument assertion from @testing-library/jest-dom:

```
npm install @testing-library/jest-dom --save-dev
```

As we've already covered this function in the cypress tests, you may be wondering what the point is of testing that functionality here. This is because we can test far more cases here with faster feedback. For example, if we want to make sure that when network failure occurs, we should see an error message on the page. Since the reasons for network failure are many and vary, testing each of those possibilities in slow cypress tests is not ideal.

Instead, a simple integration test will work for us:

```
it('something went wrong', async () => {
  const mock = new MockAdapter(axios);
  mock.onGet('http://localhost:8080/books?q=').networkError();
```

```
const {findByText} = renderWithProvider(<BookListContainer/>);
                                      const error = await
                                      findByText('Error...');

expect(error).toBeInTheDocument();
})
```

By using `axios-mock-adapter`, you can easily simulate different network issues, or even cases where the data shape changes and how the component will handle it.

We will also need to add a case to our reducer to ensure the error status is added to the state.

```
case types.FETCH_BOOKS_FAILED:
return { ...state, loading: false, error: true };
```

Fetch Book Detail

To finish our migration, we need to create an `action` for our `BookDetailContainer`, when we only need a single book:

```
it('Fetch book by id', () => {
  const book = {id: 1, name: 'Refactoring'}
  axios.get = jest.fn().mockImplementation(() => Promise.resolve({data:
  book}))

  const store = mockStore({list: { books: [], term: '' }})

  return store.dispatch(fetchABook(1)).then(() => {
    expect(axios.get).toHaveBeenCalledWith('http://localhost:8080/books/1')
  })
})
```

We can copy `fetchBooks`, and modify it a little to create `fetchABook`. It needs an `id` parameter in order to send the request:

```
export const fetchABook = (id) => {
  return (dispatch) => {
    dispatch({type: types.FETCH_BOOK_PENDING})
    return axios.get(`http://localhost:8080/books/${id}`).then((res) => {
```

```
      dispatch({type: types.FETCH_BOOK_SUCCESS, book: res.data})
    }).catch((err) => {
      dispatch({type: types.FETCH_BOOK_FAILED, err: err.message})
    })
  }
}
```

The integration test in store is similar:

```
it('Fetch a book from remote', () => {
  axios.get = jest.fn().mockImplementation(() => Promise.resolve({data:
  books[0]}))

  return store.dispatch(actions.fetchABook(1)).then(() => {
    const state = store.getState()
    expect(state.book).toEqual(books[0])
  })
})
```

And BookDetailContainer could be simplified as

```
const BookDetailContainer = ({match}) => {
  const dispatch = useDispatch();

  useEffect(() => {
    dispatch(actions.fetchABook(match.params.id))
  }, []);

  const book = useSelector(state => state.detail);

  return (<BookDetail book={book}/>);
};

export default BookDetailContainer
```

Since this part of the code is verified by redux, we don't have to test it. Our job is to make sure BookDetailContainer works properly:

```
describe('BookDetailContainer', () => {
  it('renders', async () => {
    const props = {
```

```
    match: {
      params: {
        id: 2
      }
    }
  };
  const mock = new MockAdapter(axios);
  mock.onGet('http://localhost:8080/books/2').reply(200, {
    'name': 'Acceptance tests driven development with React', 'id': 2
  });

  const {findByText} = renderWithProvider(<BookDetailContainer
  {...props} />);

  const book = await findByText('Acceptance tests driven development with
  React');
  expect(book).toBeInTheDocument();
  })
});
```

We have now successfully migrated to redux, and the test coverage looks like
Figure 8-3.

File	% Stmts	% Branch	% Funcs	% Lines	Uncovered Line #s
All files	91.47	96.88	81.63	92	
src	70	100	0	70	
App.js	0	100	0	0	7,8
index.js	0	100	100	0	10
store.js	100	100	100	100	
src/BookDetail	90	88.89	76.92	89.66	
BookDetail.jsx	100	100	100	100	
BookDetailsContainer.jsx	100	100	100	100	
Review.jsx	100	100	100	100	
ReviewForm.jsx	62.5	100	25	62.5	23,36,41
ReviewList.jsx	100	0	100	100	4
src/BookList	96.67	100	91.67	100	
BookList.jsx	100	100	100	100	
BookListContainer.jsx	92.86	100	85.71	100	
SearchBox.jsx	100	100	100	100	
src/redux	100	100	100	100	
types.js	100	100	100	100	
src/redux/actions	88.57	100	80	88.57	
actions.js	88.57	100	80	88.57	21,37,52,68
src/redux/reducers	100	100	100	100	
books.js	100	100	100	100	

Figure 8-3. *Test coverage report*

Let's take a look at what we've done here:

- Unit tests for actions, reducers.

- Integration tests for `action + reducer + store`.

- Acceptance tests remain green.

That's a really great achievement.

Summary

We introduced `redux` as the state management mechanism in this chapter. By unit testing the `action` and `reducer,` we've driven out the necessary `redux` components for our application. After some refactoring, we've migrated our `container` code to `redux`.

After the migration, we found that our `container` is straightforward to test, so we **added** some unit tests for it.

This `test-last` seems a little bit weird, especially after stressing the importance of writing our unit tests first, but if you treat it as part of `refactoring,` then that's just fine. When dealing with legacy code, we will always face a similar problem. Sometimes, the code is just too hard to test; you may need to undertake many changes in order to write a test. In this case, we can just write a high-level (acceptance) test to make sure the business requirements are always met. After that, we can `refactor` to split the current implementation, and then we add proper unit tests.

Those unit tests not only verify the functionality but also act as documentation, making it possible for other team members to understand how to use your component by looking at its tests.

Further Reading

While it can be challenging to design the shape of a store for your application, you may want to get some insights here about how to shape it in a way that is easy to extend and manipulate: `https://medium.com/javascript-scene/10-tips-for-better-redux-architecture-69250425af44`.

And in his article about GUI architectures, Martin Fowler described Observer Synchronization pattern which is pretty much like what we do in the web world: `https://martinfowler.com/eaaDev/uiArchs.html`.

CHAPTER 9

Managing Book Reviews

In any real-world project, you usually have to deal with some type of resource management. An advertising management system manages a `schedule` or a `campaign` by creating, modifying, or deleting items under some business restriction. An HR system would help HR to manage `employee records` by creating (when the company has new hires), modifying (being promoted), and deleting (retiring). If you look at the problem those systems are trying to solve, you will find a similar pattern: they're all applying CRUD (create, read, update, delete) operations on some resources.

However, not all systems have to involve all four operations; for a critical system, no data will be deleted – the programmer will just set a flag in the record to mark them as deleted. The records are still there, but the user cannot retrieve them from the GUI anymore.

In this chapter, we'll learn how to implement a classic set of CRUD operations on the `review` resource by extending our application `bookish`, with ATDD applied of course.

Business Requirements

In the book detail page, there is some key information about the book, including title, description, and cover image. However, we want something that can help the end user find out more about the book – something like `reviews` from other users. Generally speaking, a book can have more than one `review`. Reviews will be provided by readers who have strong opinions about the book. Reviews can be positive or negative. Sometimes, there is also a rating with the review.

Let's start with the simplest scenario when there are no reviews. We need to render an empty container – we'll call it `reviews-container`.

© Juntao Qiu 2021
J. Qiu, *Test-Driven Development with React*, https://doi.org/10.1007/978-1-4842-6972-5_9

Start with an Empty List

```
import React from 'react';
import ReviewList from './ReviewList';
import { render } from '@testing-library/react';
import toBeInTheDocument from '@testing-library/jest-dom';

describe('ReviewList', () => {
  it('renders an empty list', () => {
    const props = {
      reviews: []
    };

    const {container} = render(<ReviewList {...props}/>);
    const reviews = container.querySelector('[data-test="reviews-
    container"]');

    expect(reviews).toBeInTheDocument();
  })
});
```

It should be simple to make the test pass:

```
import React from 'react';

const ReviewList = () => {
  return (<div data-test='reviews-container'></div>)
};

export default ReviewList;
```

Rendering a Static List

Our second test case can involve some mock data:

```
  it('renders a list when data is passed', () => {
    const props = {
      reviews: [
```

```
      { name: 'Juntao', date: '2018/06/21', content: 'Excellent work,
      really impressed by your efforts'},
      { name: 'Abruzzi', date: '2018/06/22', content: 'What a great book'}
    ]
  };

  const {container} = render(<ReviewList {...props}/>);
  const reviews = container.querySelectorAll('[data-test="reviews-
  container"] .review');

  expect(reviews.length).toBe(2);
})
```

Here, we are demonstrating how to use the component from the outside (pass in an array of reviews, each of which has fields for name date, and content). It would be possible for other programmers to reuse our component without looking into our implementation.

A simple map should work for us. Since the map requires a unique identity for the key attribute, let's combine the name and date to form a key; in the following section, we will create an id when we integrate with the back-end API.

```
import React from 'react';

const ReviewList = ({reviews}) => {
  return (<div data-test='reviews-container'>
    {
      reviews.map(review =>
      <div key={review.name + review.date} className='review'>{review.
      name}</div>)
    }
  </div>)
};

export default ReviewList;
```

And we need to make sure the content is rendered correctly:

```
+
+    expect(reviews[0].innerHTML).toEqual('Juntao');
```

Use the Review Component

For our first integration, let's put the ReviewList in BookDetail. You probably know by now, we're going to implement the test first.

We can add a new test case in BookDetail.test.js as we want to verify if the BookDetail has a ReviewList on it.

```
it('renders reviews', () => {
  const props = {
    book: {
      name: 'Refactoring',
      description: 'Martin Fowler's Refactoring defined core ideas and
      techniques that hundreds of thousands of developers have used to
      improve their software.',
      reviews: [
        { name: 'Juntao', date: '2018/06/21', content: 'Excellent work,
        really impressed by your efforts'}
      ]
    }
  };

  const {container} = render(<BookDetail {...props} />);

  const reviews = container.querySelectorAll('[data-test="reviews-
  container"] .review');
  expect(reviews.length).toBe(1);
  expect(reviews[0].innerHTML).toEqual('Juntao');
});
```

Note that the props here contain a reviews attribute. For the implementation, we introduce the ReviewList component and thanks to the componentization, that's it:

```
import React from 'react';
import ReviewList from './ReviewList';

const BookDetail = ({book}) => {
  return (<div className='detail'>
    <h2 className='book-title'>{book.name}</h2>
    <p className='book-description'>{book.description}</p>
```

```
    {book.reviews && <ReviewList reviews={book.reviews}/>}
  </div>)
}

export default BookDetail;
```

Fulfill a Book Review Form

We can generate some static data to display in the BookDetail component, but it would be better if we can show some real data from the end user. We need a simple form for the user to communicate their point of view about the book. For now, we can provide two input boxes and a submit button. The first input is for the user's name (or email address) and the second (a textarea) is used for the review content.

We can add a new test case in BookDetail component:

```
it('renders review form', () => {
  const props = {
    book: {
      name: 'Refactoring',
      description: 'Martin Fowler's Refactoring defined core ideas and
      techniques that hundreds of thousands of developers have used to
      improve their software.'
    }
  };

  const {container} = render(<BookDetail {...props} />);

  const form = container.querySelector('form');
  const nameInput = container.querySelector('input[name="name"]');
  const contentTextArea = container.querySelector('textarea[name=
  "content"]');
  const submitButton = container.querySelector('button[name="submit"]');

  expect(form).toBeInTheDocument();
  expect(nameInput).toBeInTheDocument();
  expect(contentTextArea).toBeInTheDocument();
  expect(submitButton).toBeInTheDocument();
});
```

Make sure the <form> is displayed under the description section and above reviews. The TextField and Button components can both be imported from material-ui:

```
<form noValidate autoComplete='off'>
  <TextField
    label='Name'
    name='name'
    margin='normal'
    variant='outlined'
  />

  <TextField
    name='content'
    label='Content'
    margin='normal'
    variant='outlined'
    multiline
    rowsMax='4'
  />

  <Button variant='contained' color='primary' name='submit'>
    Submit
  </Button>
</form>
```

Now, we have to connect it to state:

```
+ const [name, setName] = useState('');
+ const [content, setContent] = useState('');

  return (<div className='detail'>
    <h2 className='book-title'>{book.name}</h2>
    <p className='book-description'>{book.description}</p>

    <form noValidate autoComplete='off'>
      <TextField
        label='Name'
        name='name'
        margin='normal'
```

```
          variant='outlined'
+         value={name}
+         onChange={e => setName(e.target.value)}
      />

      <TextField
        name='content'
        label='Content'
        margin='normal'
        variant='outlined'
        multiline
        rowsMax='4'
+         value={content}
+         onChange={e => setContent(e.target.value)}
      />

      <Button variant='contained' color='primary' name='submit'>
        Submit
      </Button>
    </form>

    {book.reviews && <ReviewList reviews={book.reviews}/>}
  </div>)
}
```

End-to-End Test

You will have already noticed that when we approached this function, we started from the unit test of the ReviewList component. That is because all of the changes, for now, are static – there are no behavioral interactions at this point. In this case, you can either start from the end-to-end test – from top to bottom – or from bottom to top. I prefer to start with the component itself because it provides feedback more rapidly, helping us drive implementation.

The end-to-end test can be described like this: go to the detail page, find the input fields, fill out some content, and click the submit button. Finally, we would expect the content submitted will be displayed on the page:

```
it('Write a review for a book', () => {
  gotoNthBookInTheList(0);
  checkBookDetail('Refactoring');

  cy.get('input[name="name"]').type('Juntao Qiu');
  cy.get('textarea[name="content"]').type('Excellent work!');
  cy.get('button[name="submit"]').click();

  cy.get('div[data-test="reviews-container"] .review').should('have.
  length', 1);
});
```

The test will fail after the click (Figure 9-1), as it neither sends the data to the server nor receives a response and re-renders.

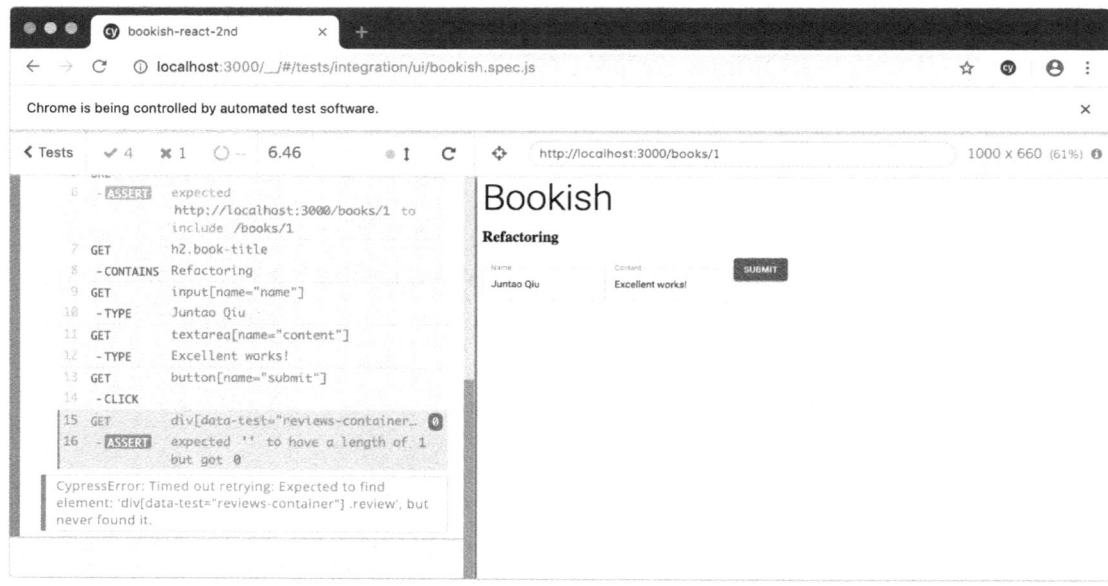

Figure 9-1. *Trying to submit a review*

To make the test pass, we need to go back to redux and define a new type of action.

Action in Redux

We have learned that all network activity and other chores are handled by `actions` in redux. So let's first define an action to create a `review`:

```
it('Saves a review for a book', () => {
  const review = {
    name: 'Juntao Qiu',
    content: 'Excellent work!'
  }
  axios.post = jest.fn().mockImplementation(() => Promise.resolve({}))

  const store = mockStore({ books: [], term: '' })

  return store.dispatch(saveReview(1, review)).then(() => {
    expect(axios.post).toHaveBeenCalledWith('http://localhost:8080/
    books/1', review)
  })
})
```

We're assuming that when we POST some data to the endpoint `http://localhost:8080/books/1`, a new review will be created for the book with id 1:

```
{
  "name": "Juntao Qiu",
  "content": "Excellent work!"
}
```

Creating an async action using `axios` should be easy for us now:

```
export const saveReview = (id, review) => {
  return (dispatch) => {
    dispatch({type: types.SAVE_BOOK_REVIEW_PENDING})
    return axios.post(`http://localhost:8080/books/${id}`, review).
    then((res) => {
      dispatch({type: types.SAVE_BOOK_REVIEW_SUCCESS, payload: res.data})
    }).catch((err) => {
```

```
      dispatch({type: types.SAVE_BOOK_REVIEW_FAILED, err: err.message})
    })
  }
}
```

Then, we add an onClick event handler in the form in the BookDetail component:

```
<Button
  variant='contained'
  color='primary'
  name='submit'
  onClick={() => dispatch(actions.saveReview(book.id, {name, content}))}
>
  Submit
</Button>
```

The unit tests for BookDetail are now failing because useDispatch can only be used within a Provider. We can fix that by

```
import store from '../../store';
import {Provider} from 'react-redux';

const renderWithProvider = (component) => {
  return {...render(<Provider store={store}>
        {component}
    </Provider>)}
};
```

and use renderWithProvider wherever render is being used:

```
const { container } = renderWithProvider(<BookDetail {...props} />);
```

json-server Customization

We've been using json-server to simplify the back-end API work for us. We need to customize it a little more to fit our new requirement. We expect that review is a sub-resource of a book, and that allows us to access all the reviews belonging to a particular book by requesting /books/1/reviews.

Additionally, we would like /books/1 to carry all reviews as an embedded resource in the response. That will make the rendering of the book detail page easy and convenient. In order to do that, we need to define a route in json-server like this:

```
server.use(jsonServer.rewriter({
  '/books/:id':  '/books/:id?_embed=reviews'
}))
```

```
server.use(router)
```

Then, whenever you access /books/1, it returns all the reviews along with the response.

A request like this

```
curl http://localhost:8080/books/1
```

would get the response like

```
{
  "name": "Refactoring",
  "id": 1,
  "description": "Refactoring",
  "reviews": [
    {
      "name": "Juntao",
      "content": "Very great book",
      "bookId": 1,
      "id": 1
    }
  ]
}
```

Great work! Also, when we POST some data to http://localhost:8080/books/1/reviews, it will create a review under the book with id 1.

Now, we can create the review via the form. Note the stub server returns a 201 to indicate the review has been accepted (Figure 9-2).

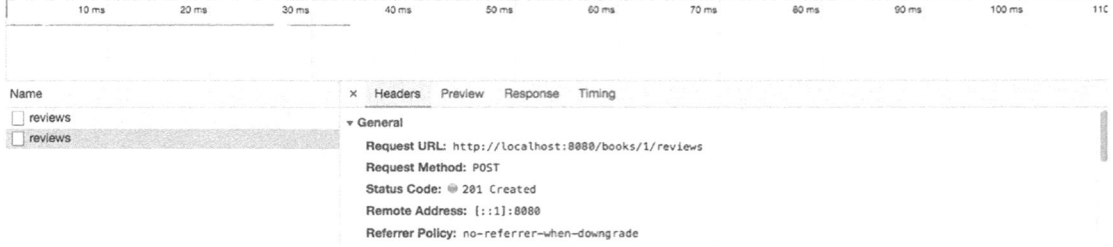

Figure 9-2. *Submit a review of book 1*

Of course, we will need to refresh the page after the submission to see the newly created review:

```
export const saveReview = (id, review) => {
  const config = {
    headers: { 'Content-Type': 'application/json' }
  }

  return (dispatch) => {
    dispatch({type: types.SAVE_BOOK_REVIEW_PENDING})
    return axios.post(`http://localhost:8080/books/${id}/reviews`, JSON.
    stringify(review), config).then((res) => {
      dispatch({type: types.SAVE_BOOK_REVIEW_SUCCESS, payload: res.data})
      dispatch(fetchABook(id));
    }).catch((err) => {
      dispatch({type: types.SAVE_BOOK_REVIEW_FAILED, err: err.message})
    })
  }
}
```

Note here we add dispatch (fetchABook(id)) in the success callback. It refreshes the reviews for us. However, when you rerun the test, the creation of review will fail because we didn't clean up after the test case execution.

To solve this problem (duplicated id), first, we need to define a map in server.js:

```
const relations = {
  'books': 'reviews'
}
```

and a function to generate the embed definition, so a route is generated dynamically by the given relations:

```
const buildRewrite = (relations) => {
  return _.reduce(relations, (sum, embed, resources) => {
    sum[`/${resources}/:id`] = `/${resources}/:id?_embed=${embed}`
    return sum;
  }, {})
}

server.use(jsonServer.rewriter(buildRewrite(relations)))
```

Now, we can clean up the embedded resources by adding an extra step in DELETE. First, we check if the resource that needs to be deleted has any embedded resources. If it does, we'll clean them up along with the resource.

```
server.use((req, res, next) => {
  if (req.method === 'DELETE' && req.query['_cleanup']) {
    const db = router.db
    db.set(req.entity, []).write()

    if (relations[req.entity]) {
      db.set(relations[req.entity], []).write()
    }

    res.sendStatus(204)
  } else {
    next()
  }
})
```

Then, we can use the afterEach to do all of the clean up, just like before:

```
afterEach(() => {
  return axios.delete('http://localhost:8080/books?_cleanup=true').
  catch(err => err)
})
```

Now, we don't have to worry about a single failing test causing issues for another test.

Refactoring

We have now finished implementing the Review creation and retrieval. Our test coverage remains high, which is great. With those tests in place, we can refactor confidently and fearlessly. For BookDetail component, the form is self-contained and should have its own file:

```
const ReviewForm = ({id}) => {
  const [name, setName] = useState('');
  const [content, setContent] = useState('');

  const dispatch = useDispatch();

  return (<form noValidate autoComplete='off'>
    <TextField
      label='Name'
      name='name'
      margin='normal'
      variant='outlined'
      value={name}
      onChange={e => setName(e.target.value)}
    />

    <TextField
      name='content'
      label='Content'
      margin='normal'
      variant='outlined'
      multiline
      rowsMax='4'
      value={content}
      onChange={e => setContent(e.target.value)}
    />

    <Button variant='contained' color='primary' name='submit' onClick={()
    => dispatch(actions.saveReview(id, {name, content}))}>
      Submit
    </Button>
```

```
    </form>)
}

export default ReviewForm;
```

After the extraction, BookDetail is much cleaner:

```
const BookDetail = ({book}) => {
  return (<div className='detail'>
    <h2 className='book-title'>{book.name}</h2>
    <p className='book-description'>{book.description}</p>

    <ReviewForm id={book.id} />

    {book.reviews && <ReviewList reviews={book.reviews}/>}
  </div>)
}
```

And for the functional test in cypress, we can extract some helper functions to simplify the test case:

```
  it('Write a review for a book', () => {
    gotoNthBookInTheList(0);
    checkBookDetail();
    composeReview('Juntao Qiu', 'Excellent work!');
    checkReview();
  });
```

Functions composeReview and checkReview are defined as

```
export const composeReview = (name, content) => {
  cy.get('input[name="name"]').type(name);
  cy.get('textarea[name="content"]').type(content);
  cy.get('button[name="submit"]').click();
};

export const checkReview = () => {
  cy.get('div[data-test="reviews-container"] .review').should('have.
  length', 1);
}
```

And now the ReviewForm should be something like Figure 9-3.

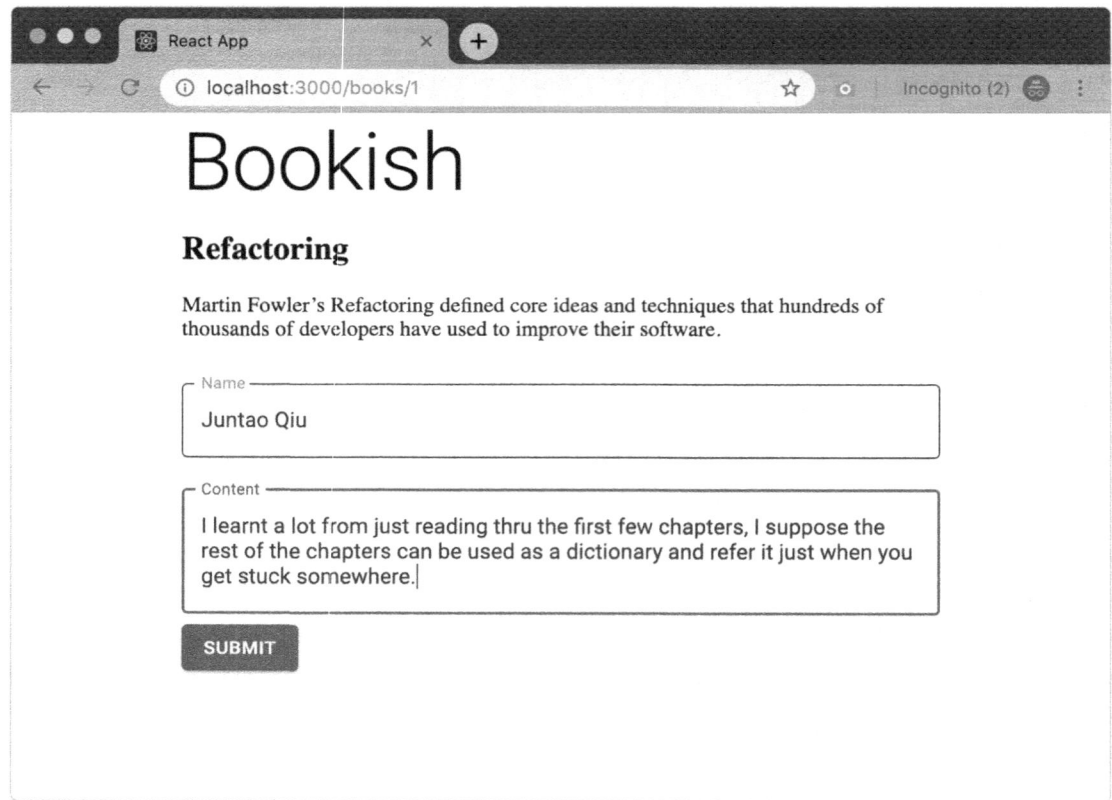

Figure 9-3. *The review page*

Add More Fields

If you take a close look at the Review, you'll find some important information missing: username and time of creation. We need to complete those fields:

```
        expect(reviews.length).toBe(2);

-       expect(reviews[0].innerHTML).toEqual('Juntao');
+       expect(reviews[0].querySelector('.name').innerHTML).toEqual('Juntao');
+       expect(reviews[0].querySelector('.date').innerHTML).
        toEqual('2018/06/21');
```

```
+    expect(reviews[0].querySelector('.content').innerHTML).
     toEqual('Excellent work, really impressed by your efforts');
   })
```

The implementation should be effortless:

```
   return (<div data-test='reviews-container'>
     {
       reviews.map((review, index) =>
-      <div key={index} className='review'>{review.name}</div>)
+      <div key={index} className='review'>
+        <span className='name'>{review.name}</span>
+        <span className='date'>{review.date}</span>
+        <p className='content'>{review.content}</p>
+      </div>)
     }
   </div>)
```

As the code in map keeps growing, we can extract it to a separate file – Review:

```
import React from 'react';

const Review = ({review}) => (<div className='review'>
  <span className='name'>{review.name}</span>
  <span className='date'>{review.date}</span>
  <p className='content'>{review.content}</p>
</div>);

export default Review;
```

and use it as a pure presentational component:

```
import Review from './Review';

const ReviewList = ({reviews = []}) => {
  return (<div data-test='reviews-container'>
    {
      reviews.map((review, index) => <Review key={index} review={review}/>)
    }
  </div>)
};
```

Since all the logic for rendering a review has been moved to its own component, we can move the corresponding test as well.

```
import Review from './Review';

describe('Review', () => {
  it('renders', () => {
    const props = {
      review: {
        name: 'Juntao',
        date: '2018/06/21',
        content: 'Excellent work, really impressed by your efforts'
      },
    };

    const {container} = render(<Review {...props}/>);
    const review = container.querySelector('.review');

    expect(review.querySelector('.name').innerHTML).toEqual('Juntao');
    expect(review.querySelector('.date').innerHTML).toEqual('2018/06/21');
    expect(review.querySelector('.content').innerHTML)
      .toEqual('Excellent work, really impressed by your efforts');
  })
});
```

In that way, it's much easier for us to test different variations of data. For example, if tomorrow the product owner decides they want to show the date in a relative way, for example, Posted 5 mins ago or Posted yesterday, instead of the absolute date, we don't have to touch the ReviewList at all.

All the tests are passing without issue – great! Our code is more concise and cohesive, with clear responsibility. Additionally, our high test coverage means we don't have to worry about breaking the existing function when we are refactoring.

Review Editing

The Review component now provides basic presentation. However, in the real world, the user could have left a typo in their review or would completely rewrite the content. We need to allow the user to edit the Review they have already posted.

We need to add an Edit button that will change to a Submit button when clicked (waiting for the user to submit). When a user clicks Submit, the text turns to Edit again. So the first test could be

```
it('editing', () => {
  const props = {
    review: {
      name: 'Juntao',
      date: '2018/06/21',
      content: 'Excellent work, really impressed by your efforts'
    },
  };

  const {getByText} = render(<Review {...props}/>);
  const button = getByText('Edit');

  expect(button.innerHTML).toEqual('Edit');

  userEvent.click(button);

  expect(button.innerHTML).toEqual('Submit');
});
```

By using userEvent.click, we can simulate the click event on the Edit button, and verify the text changes on the button. We can achieve that by introducing state to the component:

```
const [editing, setEditing] = useState(false);
```

All we need to do is toggle the status of editing. For rendering, we can decide which text to display by the editing state like this:

```
<Button variant='contained' color='primary' name='submit' onClick={() =>
setEditing(!editing)}>
  {!editing ? 'Edit' : 'Submit'}
</Button>
```

We'd like there to be a `textarea` that displays when the user clicks `Edit` and copy all the review content into the `textarea` for editing:

```
it('copy content to a textarea for editing', () => {
  const props = {
    review: {
      name: 'Juntao',
      date: '2018/06/21',
      content: 'Excellent work, really impressed by your efforts'
    },
  };

  const {getByText, container} = render(<Review {...props}/>);
  const button = getByText('Edit');
  const content = container.querySelector('p.content');
  const editingContent = container.querySelector('textarea[name=
  "content"]');

  expect(content).toBeInTheDocument();
  expect(container.querySelector('textarea[name="content"]'))
  .not.toBeInTheDocument();

  userEvent.click(button);

  expect(content).not.toBeInTheDocument();

  expect(container.querySelector('textarea[name="content"]')).
  toBeInTheDocument();
  expect(container.querySelector('textarea[name="content"]').innerHTML)
    .toEqual('Excellent work, really impressed by your efforts');
});
})
```

To implement that, we have to maintain that content in `state` as well:

```
const [content, setContent] = useState(review.content);
```

and render the `textarea` and `static text` based on the editing state:

```
{!editing ? <p className='content'>{review.content}</p> : (<TextField
  name='content'
  label='Content'
  margin='normal'
  variant='outlined'
  multiline
  rowsMax='4'
  value={content}
  onChange={e => setContent(e.target.value)}
/>)}
```

Now, the Review has two different statuses: `viewing` and `editing`, and they can be switched by clicking the `.edit` button. To save the actual content to the back end, we need to define an `action`.

Save the Review – Action

Just like the process for creating a review, to save a review, we need to send a request to the back end. The good news is that `json-server` already provides this functionality. We send a PUT request to `http://localhost:8080/reviews/{id}` to update a review. Of course, we have to write a test for the redux action first:

```
it('Update a review for a book', () => {
  const config = {
    headers: { 'Content-Type': 'application/json' }
  }

  const review = {
    name: 'Juntao Qiu',
    content: 'Excellent work!'
  }

  axios.put = jest.fn().mockImplementation(() => Promise.resolve({}))

  const store = mockStore({list: { books: [], term: '' }})
```

```
    return store.dispatch(updateReview(1, review)).then(() => {
      expect(axios.put).toHaveBeenCalledWith('http://localhost:8080/
      reviews/1', JSON.stringify(review), config)
    })
  })
```

Note that we mocked `axios.put` here. Generally speaking, when you update some existing resource, you use PUT as the HTTP verb.

```
export const updateReview = (id, review) => {
  const config = {
    headers: { 'Content-Type': 'application/json' }
  }

  return (dispatch) => {
    dispatch({type: types.SAVE_BOOK_REVIEW_PENDING})
    return axios.put(`http://localhost:8080/reviews/${id}`, JSON.
    stringify(review), config).then((res) => {
      dispatch({type: types.SAVE_BOOK_REVIEW_SUCCESS, payload: res.data})
    }).catch((err) => {
      dispatch({type: types.SAVE_BOOK_REVIEW_FAILED, err: err.message})
    })
  }
}
```

Note that we are reusing the SAVE_BOOK_REVIEW type here.

Integration

Since all the parts for editing a review are ready, it's time to put them together. We need to make sure that when Submit is clicked, the `save` action is invoked:

```
//...
const props = {
  bookId: 123,
  review: {
    name: 'Juntao',
    date: '2018/06/21',
```

```
      content: 'Excellent work, really impressed by your efforts'
   },
};
```

```
const {getByText, container} = renderWithProvider(<Review {...props}/>);
```

```
userEvent.click(getByText('Edit'));
```

```
const content = container.querySelector('textarea[name="content"]');
userEvent.type(content, 'Fantastic work');
```

```
userEvent.click(getByText('Submit'));
//...
```

Now, the only problem left is how we can verify the correct action is being called whenever the button is clicked. jest provides various ways to set up a mock or stub. In our case here, we can import the real action and then override its behavior so we don't send a real network request:

```
import * as actions from '../redux/actions/actions';
```

```
const fakeUpdateReview = () => {
  return () => {
    return Promise.resolve({})
  }
};
```

```
jest.spyOn(actions, 'updateReview').mockImplementation(() =>
fakeUpdateReview);
```

And finally, we can verify that updateReview has been called:

```
it('send requests', async () => {
  const fakeUpdateReview = () => {
    return () => {
      return Promise.resolve({})
    }
  };

  jest.spyOn(actions, 'updateReview').mockImplementation(() =>
  fakeUpdateReview);
```

```
//...
const {getByText, container} = renderWithProvider(<Review {...
props}/>);

userEvent.click(getByText('Edit'));

const content = container.querySelector('textarea[name="content"]');
userEvent.type(content, 'Fantastic work');

userEvent.click(getByText('Submit'));

expect(actions.updateReview).toHaveBeenCalledWith(123, {content:
'Fantastic work'});
})
```

Because the correctness of updateReview is already verified in action tests, we can be confident about its functionality here. Now let's try to write the implementation:

```
+import {useDispatch} from 'react-redux';

+import * as actions from '../redux/actions/actions';

+const Review = ({review}) => {
   const [editing, setEditing] = useState(false);
   const [content, setContent] = useState(review.content);

+  const dispatch = useDispatch();
+
+  const clickHandler = () => {
+    if(editing) {
+      dispatch(actions.updateReview(review.id, {content}))
+    }
+
+    setEditing(!editing);
+  };
+
   return (<div className='review'>
```

We use the `useDispatch` React hook to generate a `dispatch` from `react-redux`, and then use it to trigger a real `action` (Figure 9-4).

Figure 9-4. *Review page now functions well with redux*

Summary

Fantastic, we've finished the whole `Review` section. That's a relatively big component that has a list of `Reviews`, and in each section, we allow a user to add a new `Review` as well as editing existing ones.

Along the way, we tried a different approach to TDD – writing `unit tests` to drive out a detached `Component` first, and then detached `actions`, and finally an integration test that can make sure we connect them together.

Behavior-Driven Development

Behavior-Driven Development (BDD) was created by Dan North. His goal was to improve communication between business and technical teams to aid in the creation of software with business value. Miscommunication between business and technical teams is often the biggest bottleneck in the delivery of software projects, and developers often misunderstand the business goals, and business teams fail to grasp the capabilities of the technical team.

> *BDD is a process designed to aid the management and the delivery of software development projects by improving communication between engineers and business professionals. In doing so, BDD ensures all development projects remain focused on delivering what the business actually needs while meeting all requirements of the user.*
>
> —Konstantin Kudryashov, Alistair Stead, Dan North from the blog post "The Beginner's Guide to BDD"

The concept evolved from established agile practices, and there are different practices used to implement BDD, but at its core, it's about writing our automated tests in a human-readable language, in a way that the goal of each test can be easily understood by both the business and development teams. This encourages collaboration across roles to create a shared understanding of the problem they are trying to solve and results in system documentation that is automatically tested against actual system behavior.

Some of the practices used when undertaking BDD you might have heard of include *Specification by Example* and *Live Document*. These practices provide specific techniques that can improve collaboration among different roles in a team. They can

© Juntao Qiu 2021
J. Qiu, *Test-Driven Development with React*, https://doi.org/10.1007/978-1-4842-6972-5_10

aid developers in understanding business goals and help them to make better decisions regarding business restrictions. Live Document can make sure the software behaves as expected when changes are implemented due to an update in business requirements. It aims to prevent a situation where all tests are passing, but the behavior of the system isn't correct.

There are a lot of tools available when you try to adopt BDD as a practice in your team. What we are going to demonstrate here is cucumber, which is a powerful tool that uses a DSL (domain-specific language) for developers to compose a human-readable document first, and executable code as a side effect (by some pure magic we will address soon).

It could be used as a tool for communication between business analysts and developers who write the business rules in code. As we are aware, most bugs come from miscommunications, so having a dedicated tool for this process will be very helpful. In some cases, the Live Document written by cucumber is not executable or too expensive to run regularly. It's still a valid tool that could help during the QA process, as a guide to undertake the manual tests.

Enough theory, let's get started.

Play with Cucumber

The good news is there is a superb cucumber plugin for cypress; that means we can use them together.

Install and Config Cucumber Plugin

It only requires a few steps to configure and get them working together properly:

```
npm install --save-dev cypress-cucumber-preprocessor
```

In the file cypress/plugins/index.js, we need to enable cucumber:

```
const cucumber = require('cypress-cucumber-preprocessor').default

module.exports = (on, config) => {
  on('file:preprocessor', cucumber())
}
```

In the `cypress.json` file in the project root folder, add this line to let `cypress` load files that end with feature (by using wildcast *.feature) file instead:

```
{
  "testFiles": "**/*.feature"
}
```

One last step is to put a new section for customizing the `plugin` a bit in the `package.json` (we'll add more later on):

```
"cypress-cucumber-preprocessor": {
  "nonGlobalStepDefinitions": true
}
```

Cool, that's all for the configuration. We can now start to write some `feature` tests in plain English.

Live Document with `cucumber`

File Structure

By default `cypress-cucumber-preprocessor` is looking for `feature` files under `cypress/integration` folder:

```
cypress/integration
├── Bookish
│   ├── heading.js
│   ├── index.js
├── Bookish.feature
```

So at runtime, `cypress-cucumber-preprocessor` will load *.feature and try to execute them.

The First Feature Specification

Because you can describe your test in plain English, it should be straightforward to translate the acceptance criteria we described in Chapter 3 into the format cucumber wants:

```
Feature: Book List
  As a reader
  I want to see books that are trending
  So I know what to read next

  Scenario: Heading
    Given I am a bookish user
    When I open the list page
    Then I can see the title "Bookish" is listed
```

Note the indention and keywords like Scenario, Given, When, and Then. Some of the earlier text is just for human beings. For example, the interpreter isn't interested in the As a <role>, I want to <do something>, So that<business value> section. That part is like comments in any other programming language and won't be picked up by cucumber. Instead, it will start right from the Scenario section beneath.

Define the Steps

All the sentences in a Scenario section are called a step definition and need to be translated into executable code in some way behind the scenes. cucumber uses regular expressions to match the sentence. It tries to extract some parameter from the sentence, which is then passed into the step function.

Interpret Sentences by Step Definition

We can define regular expressions with Given, When, and Then functions from cypress-cucumber-preprocessor and do something interesting in those functions.

For example:

```
import {checkAppTitle, gotoApp} from '../../helpers';

import {Given, Then, When} from 'cypress-cucumber-preprocessor/steps';

Given(`I am a bookish user`, () => {
  //
});
When(`I open the list page`, () => {
  gotoApp();
});
Then(`I can see the title {string} is showing`, (title) => {
  checkAppTitle(title);
});
```

The parameters passed into Given, When, and Then functions are pretty similar; the first one is a regular expression, which is used to match a sentence in .feature files. The second is a similar regular expression, which returns a callback, which will be invoked once there is a match. If there are some patterns in the regular expression, the value will be extracted and passed to the callback (see the Then example). This is a simple but powerful mechanism that allows us to do some interesting work – including launching the browser and checking if particular elements are showing on the page.

Now let's run npm run e2e (as you can see in Figure 10-1 below) to verify everything is correctly linked.

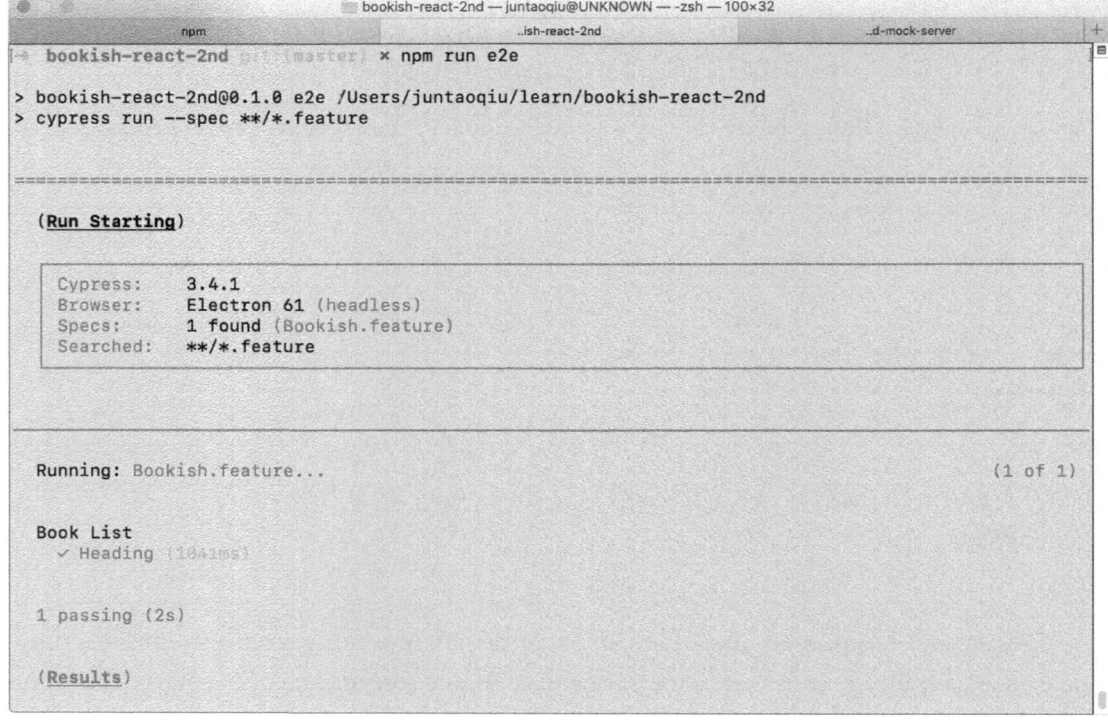

Figure 10-1. *Run tests defined in feature file*

So, our Feature is interpreted correctly, and the parameters are extracted and passed to the method correspondingly. Note that we can reuse functions we extracted in the previous chapters like gotoApp() and checkAppTitle.

Book List

With every piece connected, we can now start to define a step definition with existing helper functions.

Define Book List Scenario

```
Scenario: Book List
  Given I am a bookish user
  When I open the list page
  And there is a book list
```

```
| name                  |
| Refactoring           |
| Domain-driven design  |
| Building Microservices |
```

If you have used markdown to write documentation, you will recognize the table we just defined earlier. That's right, you can define a more complex data structure in feature file by using table: the structure enclosed by pipe |. That's a better way to organize repeatable data in your test and is both easy for reading by human beings and for parsing by code.

Use Data Table Interface

Each row will be treated as a row in a table, and you can actually define many columns for each row:

```
And there is
  | name                  | price |
  | Refactoring           | $100  |
  | Domain-driven design  | $120  |
  | Building Microservices | $80  |
```

cucumber provides a compelling DTI (Data Table Interface) to help developers to parse and use data tables. For example, if we want to get the BookList defined in the feature file within step, just use table.rows:

```
And(`there are a book list`, table => {
  console.log(table.rows())
});
```

You'll data in this shape in your console:

```
[ [ 'Refactoring' ],
  [ 'Domain-driven design' ],
  [ 'Building Microservices' ] ]
```

Alternatively, if you prefer JSON, you can call table.hashes() instead:

```
[ { name: 'Refactoring' },
  { name: 'Domain-driven design' },
  { name: 'Building Microservices' } ]
```

Thus, in our step definition, we can use the DTI to do the assertion:

```
And(`there is a book list`, table => {
  const actual = table.rows().map(x => x[0]);
  checkBookListWith(actual);
});
```

Before and After Hooks

Just as what we have done in the raw cypress tests, we need to set up/tear down fixture data by using Before and After hooks:

```
import {feedStubBooks} from '../../helpers';
import {cleanUpStubBooks} from '../../helpers';

import {Before, After} from 'cypress-cucumber-preprocessor/steps';

Before(() => {
  feedStubBooks();
});

After(() => {
  cleanUpStubBooks();
});
```

It should be pretty straightforward for you as we saw similar stuff already in cypress.

Searching

The next scenario we can test is the searching feature. We can describe the business requirement in plain English:

```
Scenario: Search by keyword
  Given I am a bookish user
  When I open the list page
  And I typed "design" to perform a search
  Then I should see "Domain-driven design" is matched
```

Step Definitions

It is effortless to implement these steps, provided we have the all the **helper functions in position**:

```
import {checkBookListWith, performSearch} from '../../helpers';

import {And, Then} from 'cypress-cucumber-preprocessor/steps';

And(`I typed {string} to perform a search`, (term) => {
  performSearch(term);
});

Then(`I should see {string} is matched`, (book) => {
  checkBookListWith([book]);
});
```

Neat! The `step` functions are almost self-explaining. Note how **we reuse existing** `helper` functions here in step definitions.

Reviews Page

Similarly, we can rewrite the `review` feature tests in the following **sentence, in English**:

```
Scenario: Write a review
  Given I am a bookish user
  When I open the book detail page for the first item
  And I add a review to that book
    | name        | content         |
    | Juntao Qiu  | Excellent work! |
  Then I can see it displayed beneath the description section with the
  text "Excellent works!"
```

Again, we can reuse a lot of steps defined previously, noting that we use `Data Table Interface` to extract multiple parameters passed in:

```
import {When, And, Then} from 'cypress-cucumber-preprocessor/steps';
import {checkBookDetail, checkReview, composeReview, gotoNthBookInTheList}
from '../../helpers';
```

```
When(`I open the book detail page for the first item`, () => {
  gotoNthBookInTheList(0);
});

And(`I add a review to that book`, table => {
  const reviews = table.hashes();
  const review = reviews[0];
  composeReview(review.name, review.content);
});

Then(`I can see it displayed beneath the description section with the text
{string}`, (content) => {
  checkReview(content);
});
```

As you can see here, by extracting behavior into helper functions, we can make the text in the step function much more concise and meaningful. Putting all related code together will also make any future changes much more readable and easy to maintain. For example, if there are any UI elements changes, we could easily navigate to the corresponding file and modify it in place without affecting other pages.

Test Report

cypress-cucumber-preprocessor provides a fantastic way to generate a report in different formats; my preferred format is json as it allows us to visualize the data in any way we choose.

Configure cypress-cucumber-preprocessor Some More

To output the test results in json, you can simply specify some options in the package.json:

```
"cypress-cucumber-preprocessor": {
  "nonGlobalStepDefinitions": true,
  "cucumberJson": {
    "generate": true,
    "outputFolder": "cypress/cucumber-json",
```

```
      "filePrefix": "",
      "fileSuffix": ".cucumber"
    }
  }
```

Whenever you run the command npm run e2e, a json file is generated under folder cypress/cucumber-json.

The Bookish.cucumber.json should look like this:

```
[
  {
    "description": "  As a reader\n  I want to see books in the trend\n
    So I can learn what to read next",
    "keyword": "Feature",
    "name": "Book List",
    "line": 1,
    "id": "book-list",
    "tags": [],
    "uri": "Bookish.feature",
    "elements": []
  }
]
```

And in each element, there is scenario execution result, like this:

```
{
  "id": "book-list;heading",
  "keyword": "Scenario",
  "line": 6,
  "name": "Heading",
  "tags": [],
  "type": "scenario",
  "steps": [
    {
      "arguments": [],
      "keyword": "Given ",
      "line": 7,
```

175

```
      "name": "I am a bookish user",
      "result": {
        "status": "passed",
        "duration": 57000000
      }
    },
    //...
  ]
}
```

This metadata can be used to generate a final HTML report (or another format of your choosing).

Use HTML Reporter

To generate an HTML report in our case, we need to have `cucumber-html-reporter` installed as a plugin to `cucumber`:

```
npm install cucumber-html-reporter --save-dev
```

And we can write a simple script to generate an HTML report based on the json:

```
var reporter = require('cucumber-html-reporter');

var options = {
  theme: 'bootstrap',
  jsonFile: 'reports/report.json',
  output: 'reports/report.html',
  reportSuiteAsScenarios: true,
  launchReport: true
};

reporter.generate(options);
```

Finally, we run the following command to generate the report:

```
node report.js
```

The resulting HTML would look like Figure 10-2.

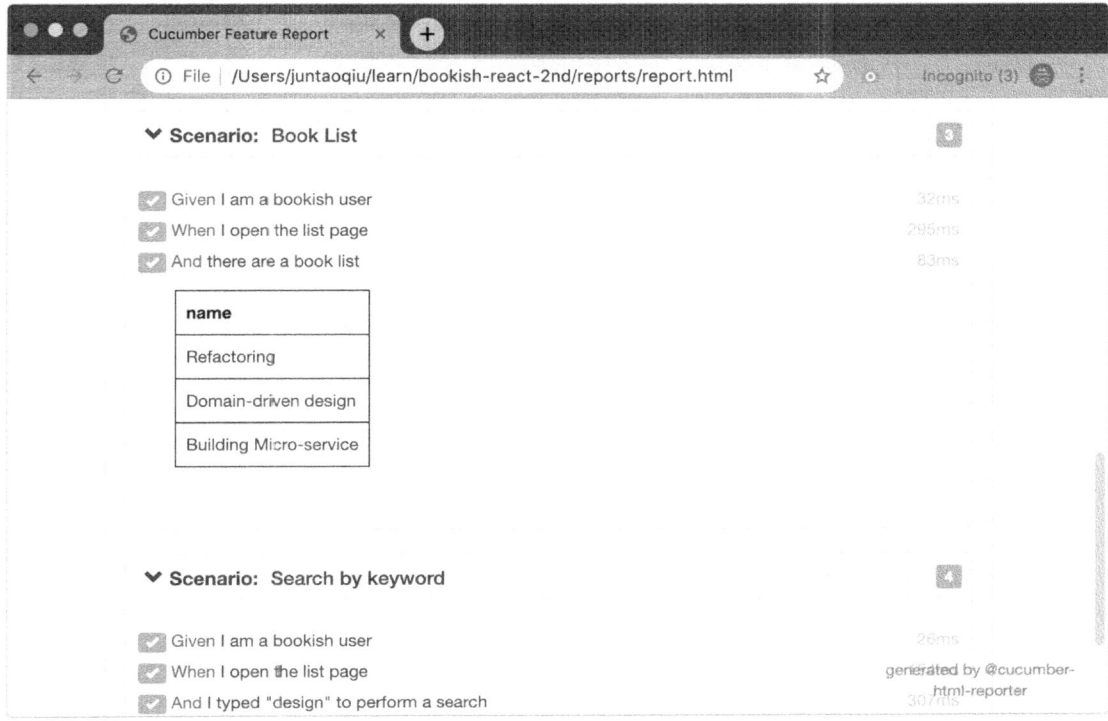

Figure 10-2. *HTML report generated*

Summary

The beauty of Behavior-Driven Development is that it allows you to write readable and functional tests for non-tech people. Traditionally, it's believed that code, even test code, is written and maintained only by developers or testers, rather than business analysts or other **interested parties** in a team. However, BDD is trying to remove that barrier and allow different roles to collaborate seamlessly and efficiently.

In this chapter, we discussed in detail how to use `cypress-cucumber-preprocessor` to write and run `live documents` with `cypress`. Along the way, we reused most of the `helpers` we have done in the previous chapters to convert the critical path of our application.

APPENDIX A

Design the State Data Shape of Your Application

A good design of your application is crucial in many cases. It would enable you to access the data more efficiently and in a more natural manner. In contrast, some designs may lead you to do unnecessary for-loops or use too many levels in a tree to fetch the data you want. In this chapter, we will discuss how we can refactor the current data structure into a new one that may help us to organize code neater and easy to understand.

Before jumping directly into the reshaping, let's first take a close look at how we handle errors in the whole application.

Error Handling

In a perfect world, everything goes well. The network is reliable, APIs always return whatever you're requesting, and it is guaranteed that responses are in the right order. However, in the real world, error happens all the time, things like network issues, back-end outage is quite often that you could expect.

That's why error handling is so essential – although there are many parts that are out of our control, we can always work something out for the failures. A try-catch pair can catch the unexpected error at runtime and allow us to try to fix by, say, retrying the request several seconds later.

Since the errors are inevitable in most cases, we need some reliable mechanism to ensure we can recover and be back to business when the error occurs. As you may already have noticed, we have many places in the code that could fail, such as fetch the books or a book when id is provided. The book we're requesting could not exist, or the request could fail by the network failure itself.

© Juntao Qiu 2021
J. Qiu, *Test-Driven Development with React*, https://doi.org/10.1007/978-1-4842-6972-5

Currently, we're catching those error in `reducers` like this:

```
case types.FETCH_BOOKS_FAILED:
  return {
    ...state,
    loading: false,
    error: action.err
  }
```

Eventually, we could end up with many cases to handle those kinds of failure like

```
case types.FETCH_BOOK_LIST_FAILED:
//...
case types.FETCH_BOOK_FAILED:
//...
case types.FETCH_REVIEW_FAILED:
//...
case types.SAVE_BOOK_REVIEW_FAILED:
//...
```

And we can expect that there would be much boilerplate code in our application. Even worse, the shape of the `state` could turn very complicated, which can lead to many consequences.

Intercept the Errors

What about we define a `global` error handling that can intercept the actions spreading and inspect the action to see if it's an error. And if it is then, we can set some flag or even inject the error message into the global `store`. Individual components that are responsible for rendering data, on the other hand, are unaware of this from happening.

I like the idea that **Sam Aryasa** shared on Medium (`https://medium.com/stashaway-engineering/react-redux-tips-better-way-to-handle-loading-flags-in-your-reducers-afda42a804c6`). And I suppose that was just delight and no invention for the existing code. Additionally, it could simplify the `reducer` significantly only to handle the happy path and leave the dirty and drone work to the interceptor.

Let's define our interceptor in a separate file; as always, let's start writing the specification first:

```
describe('Errors handling', () => {
  it('Inject error message into global context', () => {
    const initState = {}
    const action = {type: 'FETCH_BOOK_FAILED', payload: { message: '404 -
    Not Found' }}

    const state = errors(initState, action)

    expect(state['FETCH_BOOK']).toEqual('404 - Not Found')
  })
})
```

So in the test shown earlier - when the action FETCH_BOOK_FAILED is raised for a reason 404 - Not Found - we would expect there is a new field (with the key of the action name FETCH_BOOK) in the state with value 404 - Not Found to be set. Essentially, the function error is just yet another reducer. However, it would inspect actions passing through it and check the suffix of the action.type; if FAILED is found, then it will extract the message out of action.payload and put it into the state. For all other cases, it just passes it to the next reducer and leaves the action as it was.

```
export default (state = {}, action) => {
  const { type, payload } = action;
  const matches = /(.*)_(FAILED)/.exec(type);

  if (!matches) return state;

  const [, name, ] = matches;
  return {
    ...state,
    [name]: payload.message
  }
}
```

Moreover, we should clear the error message when the corresponding request is re-sent:

```
it('Clear up error message when request is send', () => {
  const initState = {}
  const action = {type: 'FETCH_BOOK_PENDING', payload: { message: '404 -
  Not Found' }}

  const state = errors(initState, action)

    expect(state['FETCH_BOOK']).toEqual('')
  })
```

So we then say that if the action is in PENDING status, we will clean up the error message:

```
export default (state = {}, action) => {
  const { type, payload } = action;
  const matches = /(.*)_(PENDING|FAILED)/.exec(type);

  if (!matches) return state;

  const [, name, status] = matches;
  return {
    ...state,
    [name]: status === 'FAILED' ? payload.message : ''
  }
}
```

And we don't care about the action that without any payload:

```
it('Pass it through when it is not a request', () => {
  const initState = {}
  const action = {type: 'REALLY_SIMPLE_ACTION'}

  const state = errors(initState, action)

  expect(state).toEqual(initState)
})
```

```
it('Pass it through when request doesn\'t have payload', () => {
  const initState = {}
  const action = {type: 'FETCH_SOMETHING_PENDING'}

  const state = errors(initState, action)

  expect(state).toEqual(initState)
})
```

That would require us to filter out actions without `payload`:

```
- if (!matches) return state;
+ if (!matches || !payload) return state;
```

The Data Shape

Currently, the state shape is a little bit rough. For example, in the `reducers.js`, we have the initialState in `listing` reducer in the following shape:

```
const initialState = {
  term: '',
  loading: true,
  books: [],
  error: '',
  current: {}
}
```

So we use this data in `BookListContainer` like

```
const bookListSelector = createSelector([
  state => state.books,
  state => state.loading,
  state => state.errors['FETCH_BOOKS'],
], (books, loading, error) => ({books, loading, error}));
```

If you have [redux-devtools-extension] installed on your Chrome, you can get a very straightforward understanding of how the data is shaped in our application.

redux-devtools-extension

[redux-devtools-extension] (https://github.com/zalmoxisus/redux-devtools-extension) is a fantastic tool that can visualize the store data along with the development. You can effortlessly understand what is going on at any time when you interact with the page, say, input something or click a button. It can track every redux action and show it in detail on the tab of the Chrome dev-tools (https://chrome.google.com/webstore/unsupported/lmhkpmbekcpmknklioeibfkpmmfibljd).

Moreover, it even gives you a chance to see in the big picture how the whole application state is or was back at any point in time when some action has occurred. That allows you to do time travel, which is the greatest invention ever in front-end development/debugging.

After a few minutes of inspecting, I decided to restructure the file structure a little bit. Let's extract the code out and put it where it is supposed to be. Firstly, we can restructure the folder as

```
redux
├── actions
│     ├── actions.js
│     └── actions.test.js
├── reducers
│     ├── books.js
│     ├── detail.js
│     ├── errors.js
│     ├── errors.test.js
│     └── search.js
└── types.js
```

We split reducers to parts that have more dedicated responsibility. For example, books would deal with all details about the book list, and detail would represent the detail page.

When given that all error handling code is now in errors, the reducer code could be reduced significantly:

```
export default (state = [], action) => {
  switch (action.type) {
    case types.FETCH_BOOKS_SUCCESS:
      return [ ...action.payload ]
```

```
    default:
      return state
  }
}
```

And detail page turns to

```
export default (state = {}, action) => {
  switch (action.type) {
    case types.FETCH_BOOK_SUCCESS:
      return { ...action.payload }
    default:
      return state
  }
}
```

You could introduce those small reducers all in one in the store.js like

```
import books from './redux/reducers/books'
import detail from './redux/reducers/detail'
import errors from './redux/reducers/errors'
import search from './redux/reducers/search'

const rootReducer = combineReducers({
  routing: routerReducer,
  books,
  detail,
  errors,
  search
})
```

The shape of the application state now became something like Figure A-1.

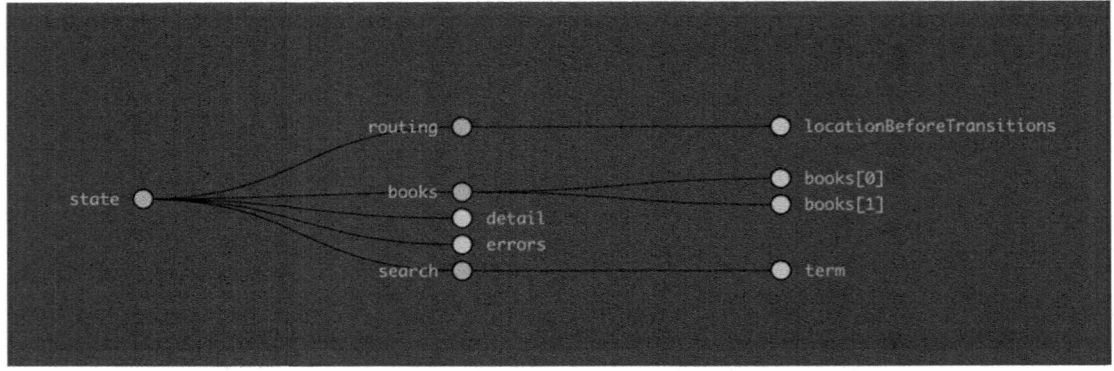

Figure A-1. *State tree of the application*

And we don't need `reducers.js` and its test `reducers.test.js` anymore. We can delete them from the codebase. Also, you have to update all the test that assumes the store to have a particular state defined as

```
it('Save a review for a book', () => {
  const config = {
    headers: { 'Content-Type': 'application/json' }
  }

  const review = {
    name: 'Juntao Qiu',
    content: 'Excellent work!'
  }
  axios.post = jest.fn().mockImplementation(() => Promise.resolve({}))

  const store = mockStore({books: [], search: {term: '' }})

  return store.dispatch(saveReview(1, review)).then(() => {
    expect(axios.post).toHaveBeenCalledWith('http://localhost:8080/books/1/
    reviews', JSON.stringify(review), config)
  })
})
```

Just remember to update all the setup steps of `mockStore` to make it align with the new data shape, and then we got an all-green tests suite (Figure A-2).

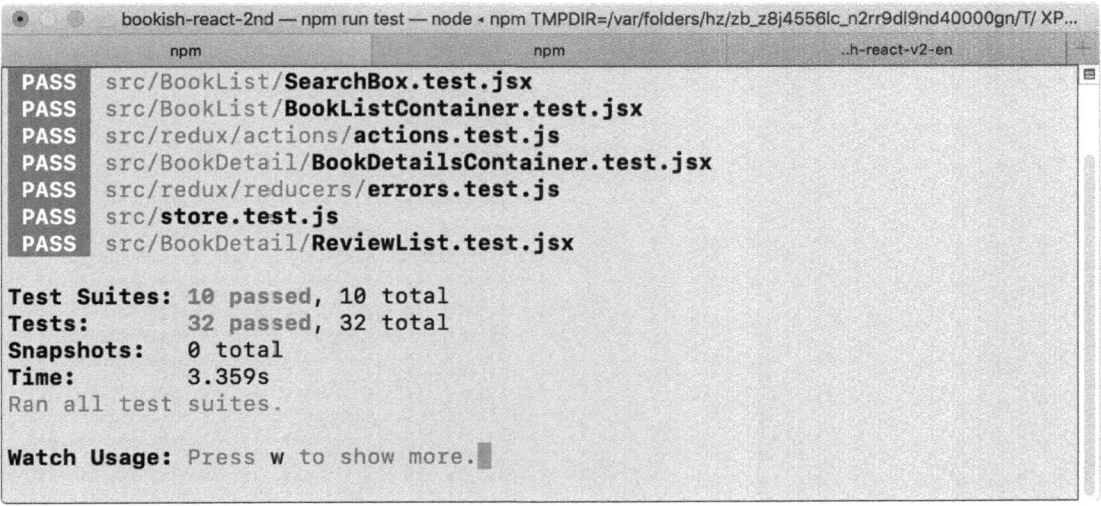

Figure A-2. *All passing tests*

Background of Testing Strategies

Test Pyramid

Mike Cohn coined the test pyramid model (`www.mountaingoatsoftware.com/blog/the-forgotten-layer-of-the-test-automation-pyramid`) in his famous book *Succeeding with Agile*. The key part of this model is that in a well-designed test suite, tests should contain at least these components:

- End-to-end tests

- Integration tests

- Unit tests

Typically, you have a small number of end-to-end tests (see the top of the pyramid in Figure B-1) and cover critical paths from the end user's perspective. And then you have a larger number of integration tests in the middle layer – those tests are making sure different components across the application can fit together and talk to each other correctly. Finally, at the bottom, you have many more unit tests that verify each building block will function well independently.

© Juntao Qiu 2021
J. Qiu, *Test-Driven Development with React*, https://doi.org/10.1007/978-1-4842-6972-5

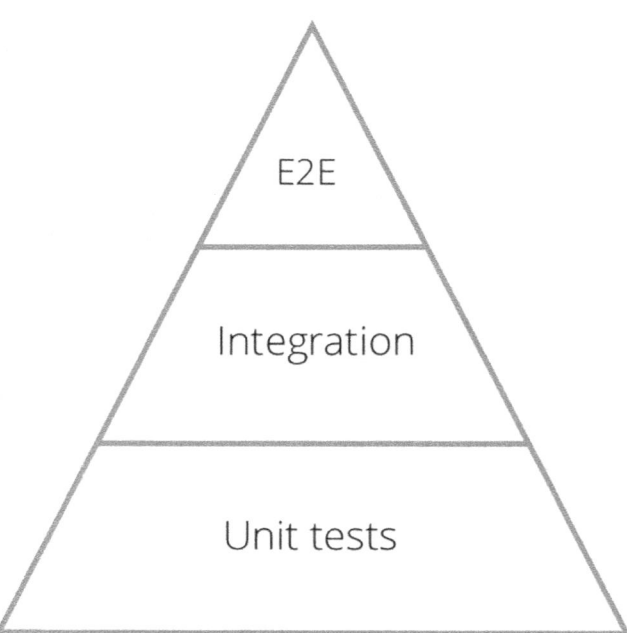

Figure B-1. *The test pyramid*

There are different ways to explain the pyramid, but the point I want to emphasize here is the higher the tests in the pyramid, the more expensive they are in terms of running cost, and the less helpful they are in locating the bugs.

Additionally, as you proceed further down the pyramid, the number of tests should increase, because each type of test focuses on a different perspective of the software quality. The number of tests for each type, the running time, and the feedback speed are all different from one to the next.

A long-running and fragile test suite does not help the development process, or even worse, it could deliver the wrong message to the team: `automation tests are useless`. And after some time, those test suites are seen as waste and then would be abandoned, and that could put the software system under significant risk.

The test pyramid is an excellent way for us to design and review our test strategy. If we build everything from scratch, that's easy. We just need to make sure when new tests need to be added, we always add them after reviewing the current shape of the test suites. In contrast, when we are working on a legacy system, we may need to refactor the whole test suite (if one exists) to conform to the shape of the `test pyramid` iteratively. We need to clean up the duplicated, long-running tests at the higher levels and make sure we have enough lower-level tests to support the development.

Agile Testing Quadrants

In 2003, Brian Marick introduced the agile testing quadrants. It's a great tool to help delivery team to categorize different types of tests. Later on in 2008, Lisa Crispin and Janet Gregory in their book *Agile Testing: A Practical Guide for Testers and Agile Teams* extended the concept of agile testing quadrants, described in Figure B-2.

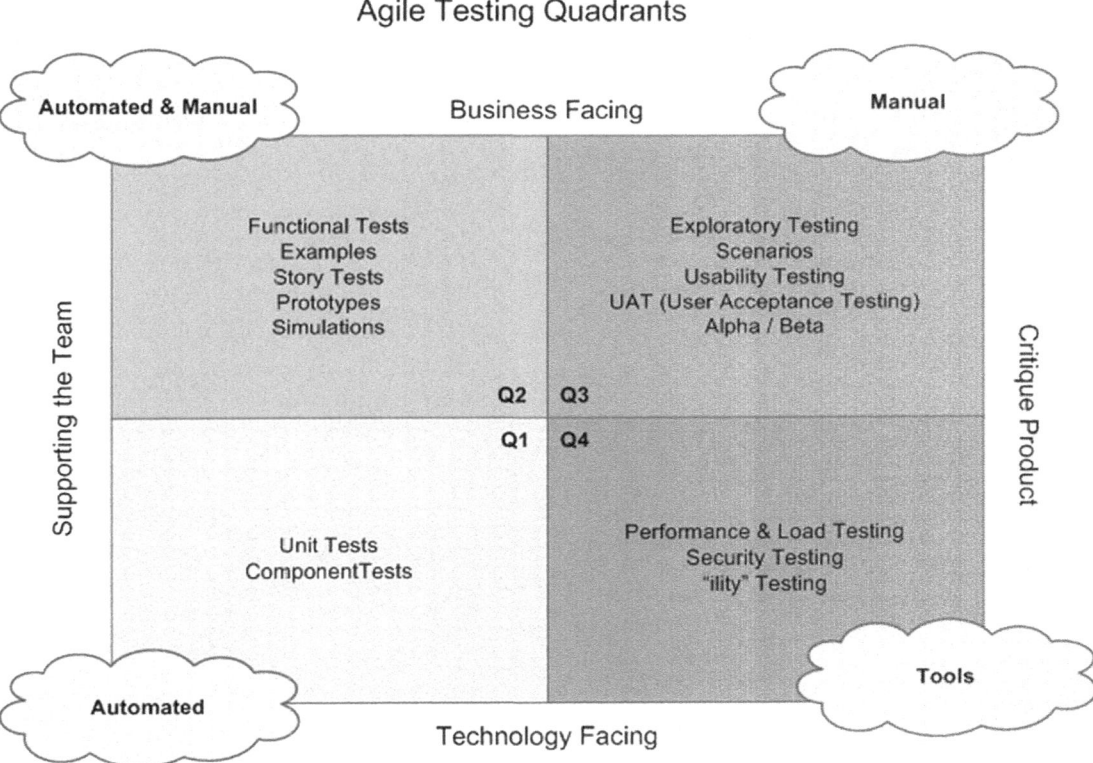

Figure B-2. *Test quadrants, source: https://lisacrispin.com/2011/11/08/ using-the-agile-testing-quadrants/*

In Figure B-2, the authors divided tests into four quadrants. Along the X axis, tests in the left-hand quadrants help the delivery team to understand **what** should be tested, and tests on the right-hand side help them to evaluate the system from the outside. For the Y axis, tests on the top ensure the code meets the business requirements, while tests at the bottom are related more to internal quality.

Since we're focusing on a `test-first` approach to understand business requirements and then drive the production code from a developer's perspective, we will only discuss tests in Q1 and Q2 in this book. In the chart, acceptance tests check if our code is meeting the business requirement, where unit tests and integration tests focus on technical details.

Compared to exploratory tests or performance tests on the right, all of those tests are used for supporting developers to write **correct** (i.e., meets the requirements) code.

Index

© Juntao Qiu 2021
J. Qiu, *Test-Driven Development with React*, https://doi.org/10.1007/978-1-4842-6972-5

U, V, W, X, Y, Z

Printed by Printforce, the Netherlands